I Got a Story to Tell

by
Authentic

APHILLYATION
AND
5- STAR SCRIBES PUBLISHING

I Got a Story to Tell

Copyright © 2010 by Authentic

All rights reserved. No portion of this material may be reproduced in any manner without permission.

ISBN: 978-1-935591-03-0

Printed in the United States of America

5-Star Scribes Publishing

"Authentic definitely lives up to his name. He keeps readers wondering what happens next as he takes them for a ride through the murderous streets of Killadelphia. He bring something new to the book game that has been missing for a long time-originality and good writing. I am 100% sure that this novel will leave first time urban novel readers satisfied while giving die-heard book junkies their much needed fix."

N.C. Manuel, Author of "My Brother' Keeper" and CEO of N.C. of N.C. Manuel Publications

"Authentic allows us to put on his footwear and walk a mile in his shoes that unfortunately led him to prison and a life sentence. Take this rare opportunity to live a real thug's life without suffering the horrific consequences that come along with it."

XXX Con/M.I.C. Tabron AKA" OG Law, Author of "6 Dreams and 9 Fantasies" and "What Eva Comes Around Goes Around".

This book is dedicated to my family, specifically those who are no longer here my grandmother – Ms. Irene AKA Granny and my uncles Freddy, Paul & Greg

I LOVE AND MISS YALL dearly and patiently await the time when I can be with you again.

Acknowledgments

First and foremost, I would like to thank my mother who has stood by my side through everything I have ever done whether I was right or wrong. I couldn't have been blessed with a better mother and I truly don't know what I would do without her in my life. I love you mom.

YARITZA DELEON: Lil sis you are my hero! You came through for us when we were at our wits end unsure of how we were going to be able to move forward. Any level of success we attain will be because of you and the efforts you put forth for us. I love you and I owe you one.

PRANK RIZZO: My brother and biggest supporter. It's been you and me since the beginning when I couldn't even really write. Those days is over and it's our time now. Only a handful of people believed in me and you were right at the front of the pack and now it's time for both of us to reap the benefits. I love you my nigga.

POOH & RONNIE: I miss y'all and I love y'all to death. Pooh I still need ya advice. You told it the best. I hear ya voice everyday. Its everyday that I miss you. Love is always goin be love I'll neva forget you.

CIPH, MANDY, MS. BARBARA and the whole "APHILLYATION" staff, thank you for giving us the opportunity to finally put our work out. It's been an arduous journey. The accomplishment means everything and the money doesn't hurt. I hope we can continue to work together.

Table of Contents

Introduction	i
Prologue	1
Chapter 1	5
Chapter 2	17
Chapter 3	40
Chapter 4	63
Chapter 5	81
Chapter 6	98
Chapter 7	119
Chapter 8	136
Chapter 9	149
Chapter 10	174
Chapter 11	195
Chapter 12	217
Chapter 13	236
Chapter 14	260

Chapter 15	279
Chapter 16	298
Chapter 17	326
Epilogue	342
About the Author	348

Introduction

I got a story to tell but before I do I think I should tell you a little bit about myself so you can fully understand who I am and why I do what I do. My name is Darnell Nevins but I prefer to be called Pooh. I am the offspring of Stacey Nevins and Jose Ortiz a rehabilitated dope fiend, ex-con and from what I hear an official gangsta.

I don't really know my pop like that but from the stories that I have heard about him it is easy for me to see where I got most of my hoodlum traits from. My story is not like everybody else's who comes from the same kind on background that I do. I wasn't born into the game. Yeah my peoples was fiends but my mom did her best. I wasn't born in the ghetto and I didn't come right off the steps and start hustlin.

I was turned onto the game by my best friend who after an

unfortunate incident would leave me alone on the streets to fend for myself. When I was left to fend for myself I figured that my days of hustling were over but little did I know that they had just begun. I was taken under the wing of one of my neighborhood's biggest bosses and taught the game from the ground up. Around this time is when my personality changed and I began growing into the nigga that you'll know when I'm done telling you my story.

What kind of nigga am I? I'm a drug dealing murderer. The drug dealing part is normal and basic shit for most niggas that come from any ghetto across America. The murderer is a little different. I hear the word murderer thrown around too loosely these days so let me clarify it for you. Just because someone kills someone else and the cops or the newspaper calls it a murder doesn't make someone a murderer.

I've seen plenty of niggas kill someone because they were scared or because their backs were to the wall. I know a few niggas that are in jail for life only because their hands were forced and they killed a nigga. I don't fit none of these categories and niggas that do fit in any of the aforementioned categories ain't murderers they just happened to have been charged with a murder.

Someone once asked me if murder came easy to me and I had to admit that it did and in a way I liked it. Or should I say I liked the affects of it. I like being able to walk on any strip in my hood and get treated like a king. I like the respect I garner from my reputation as a murderer but most of all I like knowing that I have nothing to fear in life because I have no problem killing to live.

How did I get like this? It's simple. I studied the traits of the niggas closest to me and took their motto to heart. Their motto was this, 'It's easy to kill someone. Just point and squeeze.' And it is that simple. After my first time it was all so simple. I realized that death was a part of the life I was living and that if I expected to succeed I had to be prepared to kill at the drop of a dime because other niggas definitely were.

Once I realized all of this it was over and I had gone from a mild-mannered dude to a no-nonsense murderer. My warm heart went cold and the love that I had for certain people turned to hate. I kept my normal demeanor which was quiet and laid back. All I did was add a more deadly attribute to it. I lost all regard for human life.

If I had problems with someone I corrected the problem. If someone crossed the line of respect and wandered into the realm of disrespect I murdered them. If a nigga did something to one of my loved ones I murdered him. If you played with money, if you ratted on me or one of my peoples, if a nigga overstepped his boundaries, he got murdered plain and simple. It ain't take me long to realize that murder was the easiest way to solve most of my problems. I looked at all problems in a new light. I knew that there was nothing that I couldn't handle and it made me feel complete.

I was respected by some of the most notorious killers, gangstas and hustlas in the history of my hood and I knew that I had earned this respect. I had earned that respect just like I had earned the fear that a lot of niggas had in regards to me.

Was it all worth it? Ain't no fuckin doubt. I made my mark on one of the biggest hoods in my city. I did things that most niggas will never do and I did it at a young age. I provided for my family and helped provide for the families of my surrogate family. Even though it wasn't a fairytale ending it was an ending that will always be remembered when niggas talk about the past. I stayed true to myself and my homies and any nigga that knows me knows that I am a stand up nigga. Only niggas that hate me can say something bad about me and even then all they can say is that I did something to them which they probably won't because it will make them look like the suckas and pussies they are.

So who am I? I am Pooh, Bad Landz General, murderer, hustla and hoodlum. I am the streets in the flesh. I am what rappers rap about and what authors write their books about. I'm the nigga you don't want your kids growing up to be like. But if they do grow up to be like me then at least you know they'll have the heart of a lion and mind of a General. I'm a walking urban legend and this is my story.

Prologue

AUGUST 2000

CURRAN FRUMHOLD CORRECTIONAL FACILITY (C.F.C.F) QUARANTINE UNIT B1-1

As I sit in the dayroom the smells of niggas who haven't showered in days infiltrates my nostrils and once again I wonder how it all came to this. I see the sideways glances and the cutting of the eyes. I hear the whispers and subtle acknowledgements from inmate and c/o alike and it amuses me. I am revered in the same way that a rapper or athlete would be when in all reality I'm nothing more than a hustla accused of one hell of a murder. Granted, I am a rather big hustla and I guess that's why to them I am a celebrity in my own right. What really surprises me is that they acknowledge me the way that they do and most of them are older than me. I'm only 22 years old.

I don't regret anything that has happened except for my getting caught. Over the past four months I have been on everything from the local Philadelphia news to Americas Most Wanted and finally all of the publicity had paid off. The task force that was pursuing me finally got me just like they got my two partners. The only difference was that my partners got caught right off the bat while I had an extended four month stretch on the streets.

Speaking of my partners they have us all at different county jails and I think that it is for the best. I hate to say that the love ain't there no more but I learned a long time ago to trust my gut feeling. It seems strange to me that I am having these thoughts but the one thing that I have always been is a realist.

For the past eight years my partners and I have done what every drug dealer dreams of doing when they get their first pack. We made it. We went from being your average street corner pack boys to being the niggas that all hustlas have the ambition of being. We did it and we did it at young ages. It helped that we hustled in Da Bad Landz and it also helped that we came up under the tutelage of one of the neighborhoods biggest bosses. Yeah we had some help, help that a lot of other niggas didn't have access to but make no mistakes about it we made our mark.

We built an empire. Well maybe not an empire but it was something special. We made a ton of money, drove some nice cars and fucked some bad bitches. We were hood celebrities and proud of it and there was nothing that the niggas from our hood could do about it.

Now four months removed from the madness of it all I look back and I can see nothing but the mistakes we made. The same mistakes that most niggas who get a lot of money at a young age make. I truly believe that had it not been for our mentor that we would have been in jail or dead years ago but the little bit of listening that we did do extended our run considerably.

My partners and I all have different opinions on why we ended up in jail or should I say that our opinions differ on what actually led us to doing what we did. In case I forgot to tell you we're locked up for the execution style murder of an undercover cop that infiltrated our ranks.

All of us silently point our blaming fingers at one another but the truth is that we're all partly to blame and while I'm sure that one of us is at fault more than the other two we really don't know who that one is.

I know what I'm saying probably makes no sense to you but if you bear with me I'll take you on a step by step journey with me and tell you the story of three niggas who lived every hustla's dream and witnessed the nightmares that go along with them. This is our story and I'm going to tell it exactly the way that it happened.

Chapter 1

OCTOBER 1986

When I first met Spud you could have never told me that one day we would be best friends. I was in the third grade when the skinny Puerto Rican kid who walked like he owned the world approached me and told me that I was going to be a part of his crew. Taught by my mother never to be a follower I told him that I could only join his crew if I could be the leader which would mean that it would be my crew. Spud became enraged that I would even suggest such a thing and pushed me so I pushed him back then WHAM! He sucka punched me and we fought like third graders do swinging wild punches and wrestling more than we boxed but we did land a few good shots.

A hall monitor broke up the fight and ushered us to the principal's office where we sat side by side waiting to be seen. We both nursed busted lips and while I checked the gauze pad that I had been given to dab the blood, Spud leaned over to me. I clenched my fists ready for round two but he simply asked me would I join the crew if we could both be leaders. I wouldn't be following anybody so I figured that it was okay. I did correct him though and told him that it wasn't just his crew anymore. It was now our crew.

That was fourteen years ago in 1986 and we were 8 years old. Allow me to fast forward to 1992. It was the summertime, we were 14 and we swore we had life figured out.

JUNE 1992

"You sure her mom ain't home?" I asked for about the tenth time.

"Yeah nigga now stop asking," Spud responded and led the way to what was to be our second sexual conquest.

Even though this was as we had said in the third grade "our crew" it still only consisted of me and Spud and he usually did most of the leading. I was cool with it though especially since he always had the best plans. Tonight Spud was leading the way to Jennifer and Rebecca's house. The two sisters who at the ages of 16 and 15 were considered to be freaks had promised to give us some pussy.

Well actually Rebecca had promised to give Spud some pussy but he assured me that when I arrived with him that Jennifer would break off too. Spud who was always coming through didn't have to say anything else to convince me. If he said I was going to get some pussy then I knew that I was.

When we got there the sisters were sitting on their steps looking good in their biker shorts and matching Nike t-shirts.

"Who he?" Jennifer asked pointing at me.

"Dats my boy Pooh dat I was tellin you bout," Spud told her.

Me and Jennifer looked at each other while Spud and Rebecca kissed then entered the house. I was about to become nervous with the awkward silence but Jennifer wouldn't allow it. She stood up and fixed her bikers which had ridden up her thighs.

"What you scared?" she asked and I shook my head in the negative. "Well come on then we ain't got all day. My mom come home in an hour," she told me and I obediently followed.

Thirty minutes later we were all back on the steps. The girls had impassive looks on their faces while me and Spud grinned like we owned the world. We talked for a few minutes then Spud said that we had to leave. I kissed Jennifer, a kiss that lingered, then turned and headed down the street with my best friend.

* * * * *

"Darnell is that you?" my mom asked as I closed the door

to the small apartment that we lived in.

"Yeah it's me mom," I answered as I entered the living room to find her in her usual spot on the sofa nodding from the effects of the heroin.

"Make sure that you lock the door Darnell," she said while scratching her body in various places.

I hated when she called me Darnell which for some reason she only did when she was high. When she was sober she called me Pooh, a name she had given me when I was born.

Stacey Nevins according to family member accounts had been a strong woman until she met my father Jose an ex-con junkie with a smooth rap for a Puerto Rican. Relatives say that everything was cool until I was born then came the mental and physical abuse. Ironically it wasn't my father who turned my mother out on dope but his treatment of her is what pushed her in that direction.

Ten years deep into her addiction my mom was only a shell of the woman that people described and I vaguely remembered. I sat on the loveseat across from my mom and watched as she nodded off again. I must admit that although she was a junkie my mom did the best that she could. Most of the time we had the necessities that we needed. There was no extra because all of that went to her habit but normally I had what I needed.

I looked at my mom and no matter what she was into I

loved her with all my heart. I hated that she was letting the drug tear her up but she was my mom, the woman who had given birth to me. There was little to no help from our family. Well let me correct that because there was help from the Puerto Rican side of my family who always came to our aid when we needed it. The black side of my family was a different story altogether.

To this day they all still say that I'm crazy but I know in my heart that they were racist. Imagine that black people being racist towards some Puerto Ricans. You see my mother was never the only junkie in the family on my black side. I had two aunts that were junkies and they always had help from the family when they needed it. But for whatever reason whenever me and my mom were in a tight spot either my fathers side of the family helped or we were just assed out.

'The common excuse was that my two aunts had multiple kids while my mom only had me but did it really matter how many kids she had. If she was in trouble, family was supposed to help or so I thought. I can remember a time when me and my mom had no lights or heat in the middle of the winter and the family just let us freeze. They did nothing to help us. I never understood what it was that made them hate me and my mom the way they did and they always said that they didn't hate us. I knew that that was bullshit and in my heart I knew it was because my dad was Puerto Rican.

Needless to say I'm not that close to my mom's side of the

family. I love my father's side of the family even though I'm not fond of him. The comforting thing to know is that they love me too and my mom. On the occasions when times are hard we can always count on the Ortiz's to help us.

I stood up from the loveseat and kissed my mom on the forehead then retreated to my room. I laid back on my bed and thought about the episode with Jennifer and how she told me that I could come back and see her again. I smiled then thought about the walk home and Spud telling me that we had something important to talk about the next day. I tried to squeeze it out of him but he wouldn't budge and I drifted off to sleep wondering what it could be.

* * * * *

SEPTEMBER 1992

School started two weeks ago but it didn't matter because I really had no intentions of going. I was officially a full time hustla who worked the morning shift on Hancock and Cambria. School was a distant memory.

I served the fiends that surrounded me then caught a brief break in traffic which gave me enough time to go inside Santos' store for some cigarettes and a soda.

Three months on the strip and I was like a seasoned veteran but I could remember when it looked like I wouldn't be able to handle it. After looking out for a month I got my break. One of the hustlas on the second shift got killed and Spud was up for promotion to the busier and more profitable second shift which meant that I was going to replace Spud. He trained me and it was like nothing I had ever experienced.

Within the first hour I had been gagged who knows how many times and was short $60. The seasoned fiends could smell a rookie like me a mile away. Spud told me not to worry about it but that I had to pay close attention. He worked with me for a few days then he left me to fend for myself. It didn't take as long as I had expected for me to get accustomed to things and when I did I never looked back.

Those days were now behind me. I lit a cigarette as I exited the store then walked to the middle of the block. Like clockwork she appeared. Same time everyday she never missed a beat. She would walk up and get her drugs and walk off. She never paid and we never spoke. We did this exchange everyday and nobody besides Spud knew that I was serving my mother heroin. Eventually her addiction would be the cause of me making my first example. Well that and a little manipulation from some people who I trusted.

Once I got the hang of things I worked my shifts efficiently only coming up short once in a while. When that happened I never made any excuses I simply replaced the short money with my own. With our conflicting schedules the only times I really saw Spud was when my shift was ending and his was beginning or late at night at Rebecca and Jennifer's house.

The two sisters were our chicks now. It didn't matter to us that they were whores or that they were probably only with us because we was getting a little bit of money and spending some of it on them. All that mattered was the fact that they were pretty, older and experienced sexually. At night they would sneak us into their house while their mom was asleep and usually we were there no more than two hours but it was a great two hours. "BAHANDO!"

The call letting me know that the cops were coming snapped me out of my trance and I noticed the cops cruising slowly up Cambria street. I watched as they drove past then turned left onto Front street. I went back to my post where the fiends had begun to crowd again and got back to work.

* * * * *

"What you mean I owe you?"

"I did dat bid for us. You owe me something."

"No you did dat bid for you. I told you not to rob the store."

"Mira listen just give me what's mine."

"I've already given you what I had for you."

"We'll see," the man said and Spud watched him go then looked back at the man he worked for who was staring out the window.

"Que paso biejo?" Spud asked.

The man was silent as he watched the activity on the street for a few seconds before speaking.

"Your friend works hard," the man said and Spud nodded his head in agreement of the assessment of my work habits.

"Listen if anything happens to me you stick with Rosie. She'll make sure that you're taken care of."

"What you talkin bout. Ain't nothin goin happen to you."

"Just do as I say. Rosie knows how to handle everything."

Spud looked at Cuba, one of the biggest drug dealers Da Bad landz had ever seen and wondered how such a powerful man could speak in such a manner. Cuba senses his minions curiosity and felt as though he owed him an explanation.

"I am a businessman Alex," Cuba began using Spud's real name. "I am not a gangster. My people follow me not because they fear me or because they love me. They do it because I put money in their pockets. If something were to happen to me you would see how many people would turn and join Lefty's organization."

"I wouldn't," Spud commented.

"I know that is why I have left specific instructions with Rosie for you."

"Who was dat dat just left?"

"An old friend," Cuba told Spud.

Spud looked at his watch and noticed that his shift was about to start. "I gotta go biejo."

"Handle your business papa," Cuba said watching his worker take to the streets.

* * * * *

I watched as Spud came out of the house and walked in my direction. He didn't have his normal bounce in his step. Instead he walked as if he had a purpose. He ducked into a vacant lot for a few seconds then reappeared and approached me. I was about to give him the remaining product that I had but he stopped me.

"I need you to work my shift for a lil while." This surprised me because Spud loved to hustle. He never missed a shift. Also I had never worked the second shift and I wasn't sure if I could handle it.

"I don't know Spud."

"Just do it," he told me forcefully.

"Aiight," I said and went back to my post.

Just as I thought I wasn't able to keep up with the traffic, the other hustlas helped to pick up my slack because I was slowing them down. During a break in the traffic I looked around for Spud and spotted him sitting on some steps across the street from Cuba's house with a determined look on his face.

Within seconds I was caught back up in the hustle and bustle of the drug flow. I served fiends hand over fist to the point where I had to run to a predetermined spot to stash my money. During one of these times I returned to find everybody's attention focused on something towards the middle of the block.

When I looked to see what was going on I noticed that Cuba was in front of his house arguing with some man that I didn't recognize. The argument got heated and the man Cuba was arguing with stepped back and lifted his shirt revealing a gun. From the corner of my eye I caught a movement and when I turned I saw Spud setting up off of the steps and heading across the street with his hand under his shirt.

I looked back to Cuba who looked as if he was pleading now and that's when I saw it. My first homicide. The gun came off the man's waist and before I knew it Cuba's body had jerked and fallen to the pavement.

Initially there were only three shots fired but out of nowhere more shots erupted and that's when I saw my second homicide. The man who had shot Cuba lurched forward and dropped his gun. As he looked in the direction that the shots had come from so did everybody else and to my surprise Spud was jogging towards the man with a raised gun in his hand.

The man tried to run but Spud shot him again and again until the man fell to the hard concrete. Spud stood over top of the man and continued to shoot until the gun he held jerked back. Realizing that he had no more bullets Spud turned and walked towards Cuba's body where Rosie was screaming. He looked at Cuba for a few seconds then ran off. This would change everything in our young lives.

Chapter 2

TWO WEEKS LATER

The two weeks following Cuba's murder were a whirlwind for me. With the death of Cuba Hancock and Cambria was no longer owned property. Everywhere you looked there were different people jockeying for power and it looked as though Lefty was winning. Spud had been dodging the cops who were looking for him and so far he had done a good job or at least I thought so.

He had been staying with different friends. He actually stayed at my house the first two nights following the murder. The third day the cops came there looking for him but he wasn't there. It made that hiding spot a dead issue though. For the past week he had been hiding in Rebecca's basement. Rebecca swore up and down that she was now totally committed to Spud. She swore she had left everyone else alone and wanted nobody but him. Spud believed her and if he did then so did I.

I on the other hand was broke again. Since I was new to hustling I didn't know how to stack some of what I made for a rainy day. One day Lefty tried to recruit me but out of respect for Cuba and loyalty to Spud I turned him down. Rosie seen me turn Lefty down and when I walked past her she simply smiled.

I was on my way to Rebecca's to see Spud and only Spud because since I had gone broke Jennifer had been acting funny towards me. I wasn't sweating it and obviously she wasn't either because when I got there she was sitting on the steps with some guy I recognized but didn't know.

"Where ya sista?" I asked as I walked up.

"Hello," she responded sarcastically.

"Is she here?" I asked her and before she could answer, Rebecca appeared in the doorway.

"Come in Pooh," she told me and opened the door.

On my way in I heard Jennifer tell the guy she was sitting with that I was just made that she left me. Maybe I was a little. Rebecca led me down to the basement where I found Spud pacing like a madman.

"What's up Spud?"

"I gotta get outta here."

"For what?"

"I gotta go see Rosie."

"Who's Rosie?" Rebecca questioned.

"Why you gotta see her for?" I asked ignoring Rebecca's question.

"Cuz Cuba told me to."

"Who's Rosie," Rebecca questioned again.

"Shut up Becca," Spud shouted and she did.

"Spud you can't go out there. Da cops lookin for you."

"So what. I gotta see her," Spud told me. Then as if he couldn't take it any-more he shot up the steps and out of the house.

Rebecca looked lost and as I left to follow him I assured her that Rosie was his aunt. Outside I caught up with Spud and gave him the sweatshirt that I had on under my jacket. It was almost winter and was beginning to get cold and all he had on was a t-shirt.

The walk from Olney to Da Bad Landz was quite a distance and on the way I asked Spud what it felt like to kill someone and he told me that it felt normal to him. He said that it was simple just point and squeeze. That was valuable information that I would need to remember. I told him about Lefty taking over and he gave me no response. When we got to Rosie's she let us in and turned up the heat so we could warm up. She thanked Spud for what he had done then sat down and looked at both of us.

Tears formed in her eyes and she broke down and began to cry. Spud got up and sat next to her to comfort her and in a few minutes she was calm and ready to speak to us. Whatever she was going to say was interrupted by a knock on the door. Rosie got up and walked over to the door. She looked out the window before answering and abruptly turned to Spud with a frightened look on her face.

"It's the cops," she said, panic evident in her voice.

Spud ran to the window and looked out then darted for the back door only to find that Cuba had had it bolted shut to prevent someone from being able to get in through the back of the house. He walked dejectedly back into the living room and looked at Rosie and me.

"Make sure y'all call my mom and tell her what happened," he said then walked to the door and opened it.

When the cops seen him they quickly grabbed him and slapped the cuffs on him. Then to my surprise they slapped the cuffs on me too. They put us in separate cars and transported us to the Homicide Unit and all the while all I could think was that I was never going to see the streets again.

* * * * *

AUGUST 2000

(C.F.C.F) QUARANTINE UNIT B1-1

9:00PM

I ain't never experienced no shit like this before. I've been locked up a few times before but I've always made bail before I could reach the county jail. The one time that I didn't make bail was for a homicide and even then I went to the Youth Study Center and was held on security because I was a juvenile but I'll tell you about that later.

C.F.C.F. is a hell hole or maybe it's just the block that I'm on. Quarantine is like a reception block and here you're treated like a prisoner of war. You're given a bed roll and a zip-lock bag that contains a slim bar of soap, a miniature toothbrush and an equal size tube of toothpaste. These rations only last you a few days and then you'll be lucky to get replacements.

This is only my second day here and I hate it already. I hate the fact that I have to shower in this small cube of a stall with no shower shoes leaving myself open to any number of fungi. I hate that I have to smell the bodies of other grown ass men who for some reason or another haven't showered in days. I hate that these same niggas keep trying to talk to me like we're cool or know each other.

I hate the fact that the trays they serve you are smaller than a TV dinner and that the food is barely edible. And I truly hate the fact that I know that I've got to get used to this type of environment because more than likely I'll be locked up for a long time. As I watch niggas run around and play basketball in the small chicken coop I wonder how they can be so comfortable already. Then after hearing a few conversations I realize that they are used to this shit.

They frequent this place so often that they actually have no qualms about waiting to go to court or waiting to make bail. The whole scene disgusts me. The female c/o that is working walks around the block looking in cells. I guess that she is making sure that nothing out of hand is occurring. She looks at me and smiles a gesture I don't return.

Since she got here earlier she's been smiling at me and speaking to me every time I walk by her. There is another female working the block and I heard them talking about my case and one of them said that I was supposed to have a lot money so I know what their goal is. As I watch her make her way back to the desk I catch some nigga walking in my direction and before I know it he is sitting next to me.

"What's up poppy?"

"My name ain't poppy."

"You Puerto Rican right?"

"Dat don't mean my name poppy."

"Oh my bad."

The nigga looks at me for a second as if he's trying to figure out what to say next. Then he looks down at the brand new blue, orange and white Bo Jacksons that I am wearing and I know his intentions before he even verbalizes his next sentence.

"What size you wear poppy?"

"Didn't I tell you my name ain't poppy?"

"Dig dis dog. I don't give a fuck what ya name is. I just wanna know what size you wear."

"Do it matter?" I asked and noticed another nigga creeping up on the other side of me.

"Is you goin answer me or not?" he asks.

"Not at all," I respond and he swings a wild punch that I duck.

I quickly stand up and get out of his and his homie's reach. They advance on me but I'm not worried because I can handle myself and even though there's two of them the one who swung the punch has already shown me that he can't fight.

"Y'all ain't gotta draw out here. Let's go in da multi," I say referring to the small room that houses six niggas and they agree.

I go in first and position myself. As soon as the first one enters I steal him and it's on. I take the punches from his man while I beat the shit out of the one who threw the punch in the dayroom. The whole thing lasts no more than two minutes and when it's over I have a busted lip and knot over my eye while the nigga that I pounded out has a black and swollen eye and is missing two teeth. I look at the one who I didn't get a chance to get my hands on and asks if he wants to rumble too. Being the fool that he is he says yeah, as if he didn't just witness what I did to his homie. He obviously thinks that it was a fluke.

We square off in the middle of the multi and dance around for a minute. He dances cause he can't fight. I dance cause I got to keep an eye on his man. Finally the nigga makes the mistake that I knew he would. He swings a wild punch that causes him to lose his balance and when he rights himself I greet him with a barrage of punches that make him curl up like a bitch. Forty seconds into the fight he's saying that he gives up but I ain't trying to hear that shit. I keep hitting him until he falls, at which point I begin to stomp him while his homie who he helped earlier just watches and nurses his wounds.

By now a crowd has formed around the multi, drawing the c/o's attention. She rushes down to the multi and enters the room yelling for me to stop. I look at her and contemplate continuing but decide against it and walk past her like nothing happened. I quickly go to my cell and gather my meager belongings preparing myself to go to the hole but surprisingly the c/o comes to my cell and tells me that she ain't reporting the fight.

"I'ma let y'all slide dis time but y'all can't be doin dat shit on my shift. Wait till someone else here."

"Shorty if a nigga get outta pocket I don't care what shift it is. I'ma correct him."

"What I just tell you?"

"What I tell you?"

"Come on now don't act like no nut."

"First off watch how you talk to me shorty and secondly I don't give a fuck about you not reporting it or none of dat. You ain't doin me no favor. Like I said if a nigga get outta line I'm on his ass."

"Dats what's wrong wit you niggas now. Always thinkin y'all da shit." She said walking away from my cell.

I let her go without saying anything because I'm not into arguing with females especially ones I don't know. I look out my door and notice that a few niggas are looking up at me and I know why that is. It's because I just set the bar on how niggas should deal with me. The message is clear. Leave me the fuck alone.

Sitting on my bed I finally calm down and rub the knot over my eye. It doesn't bother me because I know that it's part of fighting but I must admit that it does make me kind of self-conscious. The funny thing is that while I know how to fight pretty good I wasn't that much of a fighter growing up. One fight that I had really sticks out for two reasons. One is that it marks the day that I met my other partner and one of my current co-defendants. Secondly, it showed me that no matter how good I could fight that there was always someone out there that was better than me. I'll never forget this incident and how it happened.

* * * * *

JANUARY 1993

It was January and Spud had been locked up for close to four months. Without him on the streets, hustlin was done for me and with nothing else to do I went back to school. My mom sobered up long enough to take me to enroll in Olney High School which was a few blocks away from our apartment then she drifted back into her heroin induced daze.

She wasn't too happy that I wasn't hustlin anymore because that meant no more free fixes but hey what could I do. I started school two months late but quickly caught up. Book smarts had always come easy to me so the work was nothing. I didn't socialize with too many niggas because that just wasn't my style. Being an only child I was used to being by myself and I actually liked it so I didn't try too hard to make any new friends.

The females were a different story altogether. Not to toot my own horn but I was blessed to be an overly attractive dude. The combination of my black and Puerto Rican heritages not to mention the fact that my mom had been a looker in her day all helped to enhance my looks. It amazed me how many females in the school flocked and tried to holla at me. I got with a few of them and was having a good time, then I got caught up.

The moment I saw her I knew that I had to have her and I set about getting her. Her name was Lisette and she was one of the baddest Puerto Rican bitches that I had ever seen in my life. We had one class together and that was last period gym and that's where I made my move. She gave me a little feedback until her boyfriend walked up on us. Both Lisette and her boyfriend were older than me, her being 18 and him being 17. I was only fourteen but I didn't care. All I knew was that I had to have her.

Her boyfriend got loud during the course of me explaining what I was doing talking to his girl and suggested that we rumble after school, an invitation which I eagerly accepted. My rationale was that if I fucked him up then Lisette would definitely be mine. Little did I know but I had barked up the wrong tree.

We got outside after school and as soon as we started fighting I realized that I had made a mistake. Her boyfriend was like a wild hyena hitting me with punches in bunches and as soon as the fight started I wished it was over. I did my best to launch some type of offense but it didn't work and finally I did my best just trying not to get knocked out. All of a sudden the nigga slowed his attack and it was then that I noticed that my eyes had been closed.

When I opened them there was this brown skinned Puerto Rican fucking Lisette's boyfriend up for reasons I didn't know but I wasn't going to waste an opportunity. I joined the brown skinned dude and together we fucked the dude up real bad. Finally the schools' security came running out of the building and the brown skinned nigga grabbed my arm and led me to a waiting car. I immediately hesitated until Rosie, Cuba's wife stepped out of the car with a beautiful tan.

"Get in Pooh we need to talk," she said and I did.

Rosie drove away and looked at me through the rearview mirror. "How have you been?" she asked me.

"I been aiight."

"How's Spud?"

"I don't know."

"Why not?"

"I haven't heard from him lately."

"That's your friend right?"

"My best friend."

"Then why haven't you written him?"

"I don't know."

"Listen to me papa when your friend is in jail you always write him whenever he writes you so he knows that someone still cares about him."

I didn't say anything because what she said made a lot of sense. I hadn't written Spud in close to two months and I realized that I hadn't been looking out for him the way that I should have. Not wanting to keep up that conversation I tried to change the subject.

"Where you been at?" I asked her.

"Don't change the subject. Do you have his address?"

"I don't know where I put it."

"Well don't worry I have it at my house. You can write him when you get there because I know he wants to hear from you."

"How you know dat?"

"Because he tells me every time he writes me."

"He writes you?"

"All the time and I always write him."

"So if you knew how he was doin why you ask me?"

"I wanted to see if you were going to lie to me," she said and pulled over at Freddy and Tony's on 2nd and Allegheny and led me and the brown skinned nigga inside to a table.

"Pooh this is my nephew Anthony," she said introducing me to the brown skinned nigga once we were seated.

What's up. I'm Pooh." I said shaking his hand.

"I just brought Anthony from Puerto Rico. That is where I have been for the past three months with my family."

"I was wonderin where you were."

"I needed to be with my family after Cuba got killed but now I'm back and it's time to get things back together."

"What you mean?"

"I know you're broke and I think it's time we took our corner back."

I looked at Rosie like she was crazy. It was a known fact that the corner belonged to Lefty now and he had a strong crew with him. There was no way that me, Rosie and her nephew were going to take it from him. She looked at me looking at her and a smile appeared on her face.

"You think I'm crazy don't you?" she asked me but I said nothing.

"It's okay I know you do but what I need you to do is trust me and be ready to work when the time comes. This time we will do things differently. I will not do like Cuba and let just anybody run my corner. Only loyal soldiers will be able to run my corner and you and Anthony will be these soldiers. You and him will run the corner until Spud comes home then he will fall into place with you guys. You three will be three of the most successful guys in the neighborhood."

"How we goin do all dis Rosie? Lefty ain't goin just give us da corner."

"I don't want him to give it to us. We're going to take it but we're not going to take it from him."

"Who we goin take it from den?"

"We're going to take it from his workers when he's gone. Trust me it will be easy. All you have to do is be prepared to do what needs to be done. Now is the time for you to decide if you think you can do what is being asked of you."

"I guess I can do it."

"Don't guess, know. I only came to you because Spud thinks so highly of you and because I know that you're loyal. I watched you turn Lefty down when he offered you a job. You worked for my husband and you and Spud are the only ones who didn't switch sides. I know Spud is with me I need to know are you."

I couldn't answer, so I simply nodded my head that I was. She reached across the table and squeezed my hand reassuringly.

"Welcome to my family Pooh."

The next hour was spent eating and discussing all the things that we were going to do. Rosie had a lot of grand ideas and I must admit that I thought that she was crazy. I never thought we would achieve half of what she was saying. As we were getting ready to leave the restaurant a group of people were entering and one of them spoke to Rosie.

"Rosie what's up mami?"

"Teddy que paso."

"I'm aiight. Where you been? I been tryin to get in touch wit you."

"I been in P.R but I'm glad to see you because I need to talk to you about something."

"You back at the same house?"

"Yeah."

"Aiight I'll stop past later," he said then hugged her and we got into her car.

In a few years I would see that what Rosie was proposing to me that day in Freddy's and Tony's was not only possible but inevitable because Rosie had connections with more people than I imagined and those people loved her.

* * * * *

The three weeks after my sit-down with Rosie and her nephew were uneventful to say the least. The only thing that had changed was the fact I had stopped going to school again and I had money again. Rosie had taken care of me and done it well. In the past three weeks she had provided me with a new wardrobe sparing no expense and buying me whatever I wanted and as much of it as I wanted.

She had also gotten me my first car, a blue Honda CRX. Since I only knew how to drive a little, Anthony who I had now been spending everyday with, taught me how to tighten my drive game up and now I could go anywhere without killing myself or anybody else. Rosie had put me in a way better position than I had been and I owed her. She was like the mother that mine couldn't be.

During this time I also reconnected with Spud who was extremely excited to hear from me. He didn't even mention the fact that I hadn't been writing him. He told me that Rebecca had been writing him on a daily basis. Then he told me that she was pregnant which was a shock to me. He told me that Rosie had hired him a lawyer and that somehow the lawyer had gotten the judge and the DA to charge him as a juvenile. He told me that he would probably be looking at two or three years for the murder which shocked me because I thought that if you killed someone you went to jail for life.

He explained to me that because he was just fourteen when it happened that the judge after hearing that he had killed the man trying to defend his uncle decided that Spud deserved a second chance at a normal life. They were sending him to a maximum security placement in New Castle, Pennsylvania. I now wrote Spud faithfully and Rosie made sure of that.

So far there had been no talk of taking the corner back but Rosie had told us to be ready because at any moment our time could come. On top of everything else that Rosie had given me she also gave me a gun that she said I would need once our mission began. I had never had a gun before, but I had to admit that just possessing one gave me a certain sense of power and there was no denying that I liked that feeling.

One day I decided to check on Rebecca and see how she was doing especially since she was pregnant. I figured that I would give her a ride home from school and some money if she needed it seeing as how Rosie always made sure that I had money now. Instead of driving my small CRX, Rosie let me drive her Maxima wagon which was one of her three cars.

Anthony who I now called Tone went with me and I must admit that it felt good to be going back to the school that I once attended in style. Just as we were pulling up, school was letting out and I spotted Rebecca and her big belly.

"Becca," I called out to her lowering the system that I had been blasting.

She looked around for a second before spotting me. She smiled and waved at me and signaled me over to her. I got out of the car and walked over to where she was standing with three other females one of them being her sister Jennifer.

"Pooh where you been?" Becca asked as she hugged me.

"I been around."

"Look I'm pregnant," she said as if it wasn't noticeable.

"I heard. Spud told me."

"Oh you talked to him?"

"Yeah."

"Good, cause he always askin' 'bout you but I couldn't find you.

I heard you was goin to school here but I wasn't comin when you was. I just came back last week."

"I know dats why I'm here. I came to see you."

"How you doin Pooh?" Jennifer said with a whole lot of attitude as if she was mad that I hadn't spoken to her yet.

"What's up," I said quickly dismissing her.

"Dats ya car?" Becca asked.

"Na it ain't mine but I got a car. It's at my aunts house. Dis her car."

"Where you goin?"

"Nowhere. I came to take you home."

"For real?"

"Yeah."

She quickly said good-bye to her girlfriends and she and Jennifer made their way to the car. As I was letting them into the back seat something caught my attention and there she was the reason for my ass whipping. Me and Lisette locked eyes and she smiled coyly then averted her eyes. Becca caught me looking at her and grabbed my attention.

"Why you starin at her like dat?"

"You know her?"

"Yeah dats Lisette."

"Call her over here."

"I don't know Pooh, her boyfriend crazy."

"I know."

Becca was about to say something else when she stopped and thought about what I had just said.

"Oh my god you the one that was fightin wit him before."

"Yeah dat was me and my homie."

"Y'all fucked him up."

"You goin call her or what?"

Becca looked at me then at Jennifer and it was then that I realized that if I was going to have Lisette that I was going to have to do it on my own. I shut the car door and made my way over to her hoping for the best.

"What's up?" I said as I approached her. I hope she didn't look at me differently after seeing me get my ass whipped by her boyfriend.

"Hi."

"What you doin?"

"Waitin for someone."

"Who ya boyfriend?"

"Yup."

"Where he at?"

"I don't know."

"Why you waitin for him if you don't even know where he at?"

"Cause I wait for him everyday."

"You need a ride?'

"Didn't I just tell you I was waitin on somebody? Plus you got enough girls in ya car."

"Dem ain't no girls. Dey like family."

"Dats what dey all say."

"I'm for real. Becca is pregnant by my cousin."

"What about her sister?"

"What about her?"

"You tell me."

"I used to go wit her but not no more." "Whateva."

"Why you say dat?"

"No reason," she said looking around for her boyfriend who was nowhere to be found.

"You see he ain't comin so you should let me give you a ride home."

"No thank you."

By then I was getting tired of asking so I turned to walk away but she stopped me. When I turned around she had a pen in her hand and was retrieving a piece of paper. She wrote her phone number down and gave it to me and told me to call her. I took the number and without any further conversation headed back to my car.

After I had gotten in and turned the system back up I pulled off. On my way past Lisette I noticed her boyfriend approaching her and we locked eyes as I drove by. I wondered if he knew that his days were numbered.

Chapter 3

SEPTEMBER 2000

C.F.C.F UNIT C2-1

Goddamn I'm tired! I been up since 4:30 this morning which was when they woke me up to go to court. I had my preliminary hearing today and as expected I got held over for trial in connection with the murder of the undercover cop. The whole ordeal took no more than an hour. The prosecution made their case, presented a few witnesses and before I knew what was happening the judge was holding me for trial and the sheriffs were leading me from the courtroom.

One good thing did come out of this day. I did get to see Lisette and my three beautiful kids in the courtroom. This was the first time that I had seen them since I went on the run and it was truly a treat to see them there supporting me. Rosie was in the courtroom also but I knew she would be because that is the kind of woman she is. Since the day she picked me up from school when I was 14 she had been nothing but good to me so seeing her wasn't a surprise.

I will probably get my first visit today from Lisette and the kids. As I was leaving the courtroom she told me that she would be up to see me and I needed that. I need to be able to kiss my two little girls and shake my sons hand. I need to kiss the woman who I have been in love with since I was fifteen. While I was on quarantine I couldn't get any visits but now that I am on a regular block I can get myself together. The block that I'm on now is so much better than the one I occupied on quarantine.

I mean don't get me twisted. It's still jail and I still hate it but at least now I'm around some niggas that shower on a regular basis and for the most part steer clear of me.

Me being from Da Bad Landz is like a gift and a curse. It's a gift because of the obvious reasons such as the money we make. Another reason is that most of the niggas from my hood stick together, our hood is so closely knit that there are very few outsiders there. We don't venture out of our hood too often so we're not too familiar with other parts of the city or the niggas that occupy them. In Da Bad Landz we hustle together. We get money together and in jail we stick together or at least that's what I'm told. Either way I don't care. I'm from Da Landz but I'm my own man. Niggas know who I am but I don't know them and I like it that way. On the block where I currently reside I only know three people and I barely speak to them.

Being from Da Landz can also be a curse. There is a perception among niggas not from my hood that niggas from my hood are sweet. You often hear niggas telling stories of how they went to Da Landz and robbed a strip or set up shop on someone's corner but believe me most of it is bullshit. Don't get me wrong it happens in certain instances but it's far and few and when it does happen it's usually on a corner of no status anyway.

I've been on this block for three days now and I see the way that niggas cut their eyes at me but I got a surprise for them if they act like they wanna get crazy. They can think niggas from my hood is sweet all they want. I just hope they realize that I ain't one of them.

My name was just called over the block's intercom and when I get to the desk I am informed that I have a visit. This immediately makes my day. I so desperately need to see my family that I rush to my cell to get myself together and in a flash I'm back at the desk getting my pass. On the way to the visiting room I thought about Lisette and how much I loved her and how I wished that I would have married her when I had the chance.

If I get life or worse which is almost a guarantee, I know I'm going to regret not making it official with her. I get to the visiting room and change into my orange jumpsuit. Then I'm led in to see my family. A few minutes after I arrive, a door opens and in walks my family and just the sight of Lisette's face makes me remember when she finally became mine. I'll tell you about that after my visit.

* * * * *

"Well if it ain't Mr. I'ma da shit," the female c/o says to me as I walk through the corridor heading back to the block after my visit.

It was the same chick that was working the block that day that I trashed the two niggas on quarantine. I looked at her and attempted to walk past her without responding but she is having none of it.

"What you ain't got nothin slick to say?" she asks.

"Not really," I say as I stop.

"Coulda fooled me."

Now she is starting to piss me off. This bitch just won't leave me the fuck alone and it is getting on my fucking nerves.

"Yo what's up wit you? Why da fuck you keep hassling me?"

"Boy, ain't nobody hassling you," she said then noticed the pictures in my hand.

"Let me see those."

"For what?"

"Cause I asked."

I reluctantly let her look at the pictures and she went through them then handed them back.

"Who's dat?"

"My babymom and my kids."

"You Puerto Rican?"

"Half."

"You don't like black girls?"

"What make you say dat?"

"Ya babymom Puerto Rican."

"So what."

"So why you ain't got no babies by a black girl?" "Cause dey ask too many questions," I say and turn to walk off.

"You probably couldn't handle no black pussy," she says as I am walking away.

"Shorty I can handle anything thrown at me," I say without turning around to face her.

"Whateva," she says and I head onto the corridor that

houses C-unit.

I pushed her out of my mind while I waited for the elevator that would take me to C2 and thought about the great visit that I had just had with Lisette and the kids. I must admit that I truly love her. I know I put her through a lot of bullshit over the years but she is the woman I would marry if I ever get another shot at the streets which is a long shot. During the visit she asked me if I remembered the first time I kissed her and I told her of course I did. I remember it like it was yesterday.

* * * * *

FEBRUARY 1993

It was February 6th my birthday and I was sitting on Rosie's steps with Tone discussing what we were going to do that night. I was turning 15 but I felt like a grown man. Me feeling like that was largely in part to Rosie and everything she had done for me. She was still grooming me to fill a certain position along with Tone who was 19 and Spud when he finally came home. Lefty and his crew still had control of the corner but all of that would change soon.

I had an idea of what I wanted to do for my birthday but Rosie had other plans and I knew that I was going to end up doing what she wanted me to do. Tone passed me a blunt and I accepted it pulling on it heavily thinking about Lisette and the last time I had seen her. She had given me her phone number but as of yet I had not been able to contact her and I was getting tired of chasing her. Rosie came out of the house and sat next to me on the steps. She handed me an envelope and I peeked inside it and marveled at the stack of money which later when I counted it would amount to $5,000.

"Happy birthday papa."

"Thanks."

"Tonight we party big time."

"Where we goin?"

"Don't worry about that. Just worry about having a good time."

Rosie stood and went back into the house leaving me and Tone to finish out the blunt we were smoking. Towards the corner I noticed a commotion, as did Tone and we both stood up to see what was going on. From where we were we couldn't get a good look so we decided to walk down to the corner and see what was happening.

When we got there someone was laying on the ground covering their head and face with their arms while one of Lefty's workers kicked the individual which I finally determined was a female. I asked someone who was also watching what was going on and they told me that the fiend had tried to gag one of the workers. The onlooker told me that the fiend tried to snatch the heroin and run and I chuckled wondering what made fiends think that they could really get away among all the occupants of the corner.

I continued to watch the worker kick the fiend then something caught my eye. The blue hoodie that the woman had on looked strangely familiar. It was nothing more than a basic navy blue hoddie but the bleach stain on the sleeve was what intrigued me. I had a hoodie just like that stain and all. I had gotten the stain when I was doing laundry and the bleach splashed on my arm. I continued to look at the stain. Then the woman let out a plea for her assailant to stop and the voice broke my heart.

It was my mom that the worker was kicking and everyone was laughing at. My mom was getting treated like so many other fiends did on a daily basis and this caused me to black out. I sucka punched the nigga who was kicking my mom and before anyone knew what was happening he had fallen and I was stomping him and doing my best to stomp his brains into the sidewalk. One of his niggas tried to grab me but Tone was having none of that and was immediately on him. Seeing the way that we were fucking those two up no one else tried to jump into the fight.

The nigga that I was fighting was getting stomped so bad that Tone had to stop what he was doing and rush over to stop me. He grabbed me and pulled me away from the nigga but I wasn't done so I began wrestling with Tone trying to get away from him but he was too strong. Finally I calmed down and he loosened his grip on me.

Using this to my advantage I wiggled out of his grasp and pulled my gun off of my waist. As soon as niggas seen the gun they began to back away from the scene and Tone stood in front of me stopping me from pulling the trigger.

"Pooh put the gun away," Tone told me.

"Fuck dat dis nigga goin die."

"Yo you trippin. Yo it's too many people out here."

"Get out my way Tone," I yelled.

"Put the gun down," a female voice said sternly.

I looked to my left and Rosie was standing there looking at me with fire in her eyes.

"Dis nigga gotta die Rosie."

"I said put the gun down," she told me more forcefully this time.

I had never seen her look like that before and had never had her talk to me like that. From my observations Rosie had always been sweet and caring and soft spoken but here she was showing me a totally different side of her. It took a minute but I finally lowered the gun and put it back on my waist.

I walked over to my mom who was sitting on the ground Indian-style with her head in her lap. I grabbed her by the arm and helped her to her feet and walked her towards my car. As

I passed Rosie and Tone they fell into step behind me and when we were out of earshot of the niggas on the corner Rosie caught up to me.

"Why you help her?" she asked me.

"Because I had to."

"Had to for what? Do you realize that you almost killed somebody in front of a whole bunch of witnesses?"

"I said I had to Rosie."

"Well you better tell me why," she said and grabbed my arm to stop me from walking.

"Because she my mom," I said looking Rosie directly in her eye.

I could see the shock on her face as she processed what I told her. She was at a loss for words and I knew it so I just continued to look at her while holding my mom's arm to keep her steady.

"Your mom," Rosie finally muttered.

"Yeah."

"Pooh, I'm sorry. I didn't know."

"It's cool. Look I gotta get her home."

"Alright Tone you go with him and when you get her there make sure you come right back."

"Rosie I don't know if I feel like partying tonight."

"I understand you in a bad mood now but tonight ain't just about your birthday. It's about more than that so make sure you come right back understand?"

"Yeah I understand," I said knowing that Rosie was serious.

* * * * *

Tone sat in my living room while I sat on the side of my mom's bed and looked down at her slightly battered face. It broke my heart to see her in this condition and it made my blood boil to know that the niggas who did it to her were still breathing. I said niggas because even though only one of the niggas on the corner touched my mom I felt as though all of them were responsible. My mom's eyes fluttered open and she looked at me and smiled.

"Hey baby."

"What's up mom. How you feelin?"

"I'm alright baby."

"What was you doin mom? Why you ain't ask me? You know I would have gave you da money."

"Oh baby this ain't nothing."

"It is mom. Dem dudes would have hurt you if I ain't stop em."

"I would have been alright."

"No you wouldn't have. Dey might have killed you."

"Oh baby you worry too much."

I looked at my mom with disbelief as she made light of what had happened to her like it was no big deal. Had I known then what I know now I would have forced her to get better but I was too young to know what to do. All I knew was that my mom was overcome with the drug that had a hold on her and I felt that there was nothing I could do. When I realized that there was something that I could do for her it would be way too late.

I got up off of her bed and straightened my clothes preparing myself to leave and she called my name. I looked down into my mom's face which still held faint traces of her once flourishing beauty and hoped that she would say something to make me stay and help her but that didn't happen. Instead she just asked me for some money. I took twenty dollars out of my pocket and laid it on the table next to her bed then turned and walked out of the room. I got Tone from the living room and we left heading back to Rosie's.

* * * * *

The incident with my mom had been ruining my birthday.

When we first got back to Rosie's she tried totalk to me but I didn't feel like talking. The incident with my mom had me pissed off. It wasn't until me and Tone had left my apartment that I realized that my mom hadn't even wished me a happy birthday. Rosie could sense that I wasn't in a talking mood so instead she made me get in her Lexus and she took me and Tone to dinner.

Dinner would have actually been quite enjoyable if not for the fact that all throughout the sitting all I kept seeing was the nigga kicking my mom. I hardly ate and even though she noticed it, Rosie said nothing. She just continued to talk to me and Tone who was always quiet. She carried on a conversation with us without us having to answer and it didn't seem to bother her. After dinner she paid the bill and we all got back into the Lexus and headed for our next destination.

We ended up at Bottoms Up on 5th and Wyoming. Well actually we weren't in the strip club side. We were on the small restaurant side which Rosie said her uncle owned. It must have been true because when we entered she was received as if she was royalty. People called her name and stood to hug and kiss her and everybody that greeted her had to greet us because she made sure that she introduced me and Tone to everyone.

Me and Rosie sat at one of the small tables while Tone ventured to one of the pool tables to try and get a game in. Rosie sat across from me and a few minutes later her uncle came over and asked us what we wanted to drink. I had never drunk anything other than a forty so I wasn't sure what I should say but Rosie helped me out.

She ordered a rum and coke for herself and a Hennessey for me. I didn't even know what Hennessey was until that night but because of Rosie this would be my drink of choice whenever I indulged in liquor. When our drinks came Rosie sipped hers then looked at me seriously.

"Pooh I know you're pissed but you have to remember that we have a goal to achieve. Now I'm not saying that you can't kill the guy that hurt your mother. I would never say that because he deserves to die. I just want you to understand that it couldn't be done the way you wanted to do it."

I sipped the drink and felt it burn my chest while I listened to Rosie and what she was saying.

"If you want to kill him then I support your decision. Just make sure you do it right so it can't come back to haunt you like it did Spud."

Just hearing her say Spud's name made me miss his presence. Spud had been present for all of my birthdays since I was eight. In fact my 11th and 12th birthdays were financed by his mom because my mom was too high to remember, sort of like today. I looked around and felt lonely all of a sudden. Rosie must have noticed it because she came over and sat next to me and put her arm around me.

"Don't worry everything will be alright. You're with family now and we'll always be here for you."

Her soothing voice and her arm around me had a comforting effect on me and slowly but surely my body began to relax and I loosened up. I'm sure the liquor had something to do with it too. My fifth drink had just arrived and now me and Rosie were laughing and joking and I was actually enjoying my birthday. The door to the establishment opened and I looked in that direction and at that moment my birthday got so much better.

Four females filed into the small restaurant and the third one was my dream girl. She looked different than she did in school and I guessed that that was because she was out for a night on the town. I kept my eyes locked on her and Rosie followed my gaze to its point of focus. She looked at Lisette then she looked at me and smiled a knowing smile. She put her arm back around me and leaned in to whisper in my ear.

"Call her over papa," she told me.

I waited until Lisette had made her way towards where we were sitting and when she was in earshot I called out to her. She looked up at me and a smile appeared on her face but it quickly vanished when she saw Rosie with her arm around me. I waved her over and she hesitated before approaching the table.

"What's up?" I asked her.

"Nothin just chillin wit my girls," she said and glanced at Rosie as if to ask me who she was.

Not one to miss anything Rosie caught the look Lisette gave me and stood and extended her hand. "Hi, I'm Rosie, Pooh's aunt."

Lisette didn't say anything but she did shake Rosie's hand. Rosie excused herself and made her way over to where Tone was busy kicking ass on the pool table, leaving me and Lisette alone.

"Wanna sit down?" I asked her.

"I should go chill with my girls."

"Dey look like dey aiight," I said pointing to her friends who were at a table with some older guys.

She looked over at them then with a look on her face that showed that she had given in. She sat across from me. As soon as she sat down I delved right into conversation. Now for my age I was a smooth dude. I don't know where I got it from but I had it and talking to a female was nothing for me. Tonight was something different though. It was as if the liquor had turned me into the smoothest nigga on the face of the earth. Ten minutes into our conversation I had her smiling from ear to ear and within a half hour she was sitting next to me with her legs draped over mine staring into my eyes.

I continued to drink with no hassle from the bartender

which showed her that I was obviously someone of status because she knew that I wasn't old enough to drink. She actually didn't know how old I was and when she found out a few minutes later it would shock her and almost fuck up my chances of making her mine.

She watched me sip on my drink then sipped the Corona that she had been nursing for the past fifteen minutes. We talked a little while longer then she finally got around to asking the question that I knew was inevitably coming. It was the question that I knew would make or break me with what I was trying to accomplish.

"How old is you Pooh?"

I took another sip of my drink and told her straight out. "I just turned fifteen today," I said as if it should be no big deal.

"You just turned fifteen," she said and took her legs off of mine and sat up straight in her chair.

"Yup. Is dat a problem?"

"You know how old I am?"

"What 16, 17."

"I'm 18."

"So."

"Pooh you too young for me."

"No I ain't."

"Yes you is."

"How old is ya boyfriend?"

"17 and he ain't my boyfriend no more."

"Why not?"

"Cause he ain't."

"He ain't ya boyfriend no more cause you know you wanted me to be ya boyfriend."

"Whateva dat still don't change da fact dat you too young for me."

"How many niggas my age you know dat act like me? If I wouldn't have told you I was fifteen you woulda thought I was ya age right?"

"Maybe."

"Ain't no maybe. I'm right and you know it." "Pooh listen . . ." I never let her get the rest of her sentence out.

I grabbed her by her shirt and pulled her close to me and before she could object I was kissing her. Without hesitation she returned the kiss and our lips locked for about a minute before she finally pulled away. Her face was surprised and she was blushing. She looked at me but didn't speak so neither did

I. I simply picked up my drink and swallowed the last of it. I cut my eyes around the small restaurant and noticed that Rosie was looking at us smiling and Lisette's girlfriends were looking in our direction obviously talking about what they had just seen.

"Still think I'm too young?" I asked her.

"Of course. Just cause you can kiss don't mean you grown," she said and grabbed my hand. "I ain't into games Pooh. I'm too old for dat. You can't treat me like dem otha little girls you be wit."

"I don't be messin wit no little girls."

"I'm just telling you. If you goin be wit me den be wit me but don't try to play me cause I ain't havin dat."

"You ain't gotta worry bout none of dat," I said and she swung her legs back onto mine.

"I ain't goin worry cause if you try to play me I'm leavin you papi and dats da truth. Just ask my last boyfriend."

For the next hour me and Lisette sat and got better acquainted with each other. We drank and kissed then repeated the process allover again. At one point her friends came over and introduced themselves and Lisette introduced me as her boyfriend. While her friends were at the table with us Tone came over and he and one of the friends hit it off immediately and soon they had gotten up from the table and gone outside to be alone. Lisette was getting ready to leave because she had to go to school the following day and she asked me was I going to be there and I told her no.

I could sense that she wanted to ask me why but she didn't. Instead she told me to pick her up after school which I instantly agreed to do. Then she stood up. I stood with her. She wrapped her arms around my neck and kissed me long and deep and when we broke the embrace she put her lips to my ear.

"You mine now papi, remember dat. I get jealous so don't have me fightin no bitches over you cause after I whip dey ass I'ma whip ya ass. Den I'm leavin."

"Same thing go for you," I told her and when she pulled back she was smiling.

"See you tomorrow," she said and headed for the exit.

When she reached the door it opened from the outside and in walked three niggas. These weren't just any three niggas though and while I didn't know any of them personally their reputations preceded them. Teddy, Miz and Boo were the talk of my hood at the time. They weren't the only niggas making some noise, it was just that they were making more noise than anyone else.

I watched as Teddy said something to Lisette then I saw her blush and point at me. Teddy said something else then held the door for her and her friends to exit. As he walked past me he complimented me on what a beautiful girl I had then went to greet Rosie with a hug and a kiss.

Teddy was a few years older than me at the time. He may have had me by four or five years. His name struck fear in the hearts of niggas all over Da Bad Landz. He wasn't from my side of the hood. Seventh and Indiana was his strip but he could have had a corner wherever he wanted.

Like I said I didn't know any of them personally but I did know what I had heard about them. Teddy was rumored to be the most vicious. Word was that he, like me, wasn't from Da Bad Landz but he had been, hustlin there since he was young. He was well respected by all of the bosses in the neighborhood and feared by them too even though he was younger than all of them. From what I had heard he had killed an entire family when he was only sixteen and had beaten the case. There were rumors of numerous other murders that he had committed or been involved with and the consensus was the same no matter who you heard it from. Teddy was not a nigga to be fucked with. What I did know was that his corner was doing crazy numbers and that he was close to rich at a young age if he wasn't already.

Miz was Teddy's right hand man and you rarely saw one without the other. Word was that Miz had put a little work in but was nothing like Teddy. Truthfully a lot of people said that he only got the respect that he did for one reason only and that was because he was Teddy's man. Whatever it was he was another nigga that nobody fucked with.

Boo was a different story. He was from Da Bad Landz whereas Teddy and Miz weren't. From what I gathered Boo was just a loyal soldier. He worked for Teddy and Miz but they treated him like an equal and I assume that they did because of how much work Boo had put in. Boo was feared almost as much as Teddy if not as much. Boo was a soldier plain and simple and a good one.

These were the three niggas that walked into the restaurant that night and now they were sitting with Rosie talking as if they were long lost friends. Tone finally came back in and sat down at the table with me. As usual he was quiet which didn't bother me because I knew that when he had something to say that he would. By now I was drunk and was getting tired but I had come with Rosie in her car and couldn't leave until she was ready.

Twenty minutes later Rosie stood as did Teddy, Miz and Boo. She hugged all of them then they headed towards our table. They stopped and Rosie motioned to me and Tone.

"Teddy these are my nephews Anthony and Pooh," she said and Teddy extended his hand to Tone first then to me.

"My bad young buck I ain't know dat was ya girl earlier. I ain't mean no disrespect," Teddy said as he held my hand in a firm handshake.

"It's cool," I responded as he let my hand go.

Teddy turned to Rosie and hugged her again. Then he and his homies made their way out of the restaurant. When they were gone Rosie ordered a round of drinks for me, her and Tone. I wasn't sure if I could take another one but Rosie slid the drink to me then held hers up in the air.

"I hope y'all had fun tonight because tomorrow we go back to work," she said and downed her drink and me and Tone did the same.

"Tomorrow?" I asked after I had ingested my drink.

"Yeah tomorrow."

CHAPTER 4

OCTOBER 2000

C.F.C.F UNIT C2-1

As I step out of my cell I look around the crowded dayroom for Joe but can't find him. Figuring that he's outside in the small courtyard playing handball, I venture out there to find him. I don't want to interrupt the game so I lounge up against a wall and wait for it to be over.

Three months into this shit and I'm still not accustomed to it. I can't get used to living with another nigga 24/7. I can't get used to the bullshit that they feed us and I can't get used to hearing all the bullshit war stories that these niggas swap on a regular basis.

Don't get me wrong. There are some dudes who were about something on the streets but the majority of the niggas in here were workers or niggas who think that they were bosses but in all reality just barely making it. On several occasions I have had niggas who don't even know me try to cut into me for whatever reason but I brush them off as fast as I can. These niggas don't even know me. All they know is what they heard which could all be lies.

Instances like this just show me that these niggas are vultures who will try to get next to a nigga who can possibly do something for them. I could be a rat or a fake or anything but they wouldn't care because when they see me all they see is the means to an end.

The game of handball is finally over and Joe walks off the court. I call out to him and he comes over to me. Joe is from my hood and at one point used to hustle for me, Spud and Tone but he wasn't the type of worker that we were used to dealing with so he had to go.

With some of his recent actions the nigga has validated our letting him go. For the past couple days he's been running around the block putting all of my personal business out to these niggas and bragging about how I'm his man. What he doesn't realize is that he's only making himself look like a fool to whoever he's bragging to because I don't even associate with him.

How can you possibly call a nigga ya man and he don't even talk to you. Some people is so stupid. He walks over and I drape my arm over his shoulder and lead him onto the block.

As we enter I catch the same female c/o watching me and I realize that no matter where I go I can't shake her.

She's always there. I put that out of my mind for a minute and focus on Joe.

"Yo dog why you runnin round tellin deez clowns my business?"

"Huh?" Joe asks surprised that I know what he's been doing.

"I asked why you puttin my business out to niggas?"

"I ain't tell nobody ya business."

"Don't lie cause a nigga already told me."

"Pooh man I was just givin you ya props."

"I don't need you to give me no props nigga. I know who I am."

"Na it wasn't like date. We was just talkin bout what niggas in the city was real and I mentioned ya name."

"For what?"

"I was just lettin dem niggas know dat our hood got some real niggas."

"Yo dig dis. I don't need you to tell niggas who I am. Dat

shit don't impress me."

"Pooh why you trippin?"

"I'm trippin cause you talk too fuckin much and now niggas know my business dat shouldn't all because you wanted to act like a fuckin groupie," I say raising my voice.

We are now in the dayroom and I know people had heard me and that was my goal. I wanted to embarrass him hoping that he would learn to keep his mouth shut in regards to things that had nothing to do with him.

"Pooh why you all loud?" Joe asks me becoming embarrassed.

"Oh you don't like niggas being all in ya business do ya? You don't want nobody to know dat da nigga you claim is ya man ain't and you don't want nobody to hear me checking you like da nut dat you is," I say loud enough for everyone to hear.

"I ain't no nut," Joe says while trying to pull away from me.

I grab him by the back of his neck and hold him in place because whether he wanted a lesson or not he was about to get one. The next time he was in conversation he would think twice about mentioning my name.

"Keep my fuckin name out ya mouth and stop frontin and tellin niggas dat I'm ya man. Nigga you could neva be my man.

You ain't nothin but some nigga who used to work for me till I fired ya nut-ass," I tell him and quickly slap the shit out of him in front of the entire dayroom.

Joe jumped back away from me when I smacked him and I stood there waiting to see if he wanted to take the altercation any further. Instead of being a real man and taking me to task about what I had done he simply stood there with his hand on his cheek looking at me like I was crazy. I stand there for a few seconds longer, then I walk past him and head to my cell.

When I reach my cell I wave to the c/o to open my door and she just looks at me for a for a minute with a weird smile on her face then finally she buzzes my cell door and I enter. I look out my door and I see a few niggas looking up in my direction but most of them are staring at Joe who is still standing there looking stupid. I look at the c/o who is now coming towards my cell and I know that she is going to have something to say so I prepare myself. She opens the door with her key and I step back as she takes up position in my doorway.

"You up to ya shit again huh?" she says.

"I don't know what you talkin bout."

"Why we always gotta go through dis?

"Go through what?"

"Can we just have a normal conversation?"

"I don't have normal conversations with c/o's," I tell her.

"Why not?"

"Why should I? I'm a criminal and you da one dats pose to look over me. We really ain't got too much in common unless we goin be on da same side."

"What you mean on da same side?"

"How long you been a c/o?"

"Four years."

"Den you know what I'm talkin bout. Let's not act stupid wit each other."

"So what you tryin to say?"

"I'm sayin dat if we can't help each otha den it ain't no reason for us to keep havin deez conversations."

"And how we pose to help each other?"

"You got something you need?" I asked, knowing that she does.

"Yeah I need something."

"What?"

"You."

"Excuse me."

"I want you nigga."

This threw me for a loop. When I asked her did she need something I was thinking more along the lines of money. After all I am a hustla. But her saying she wanted me was even better because this meant that I would be able to get whatever I wanted with no problem.

"What I get out da deal?" I ask and she looks me up and down and licks her lips.

"Anything you want."

Rosie who pretty much schooled me to everything, once told me that when a woman was into me that I had to set the tone and let the woman know that it was all about me and that it was a privilege to be with me. Remembering what Rosie had told me I knew that I had to play this right so the c/o would know who was in charge. I knew that I had to seize the opportunity and see how far she was willing to go so I decided to go hard right out of the gate.

"Aiight dig dis. I'ma give you a address to go to and when da woman answers da door tell her who you is and what you do. Tell her you there for Pooh. She goin

give you something for me and I need dat A.S.A.P."

"Aiight give me da address," she said with no hesitation. So

I wrote down Rosie's address and handed it to her.

"What about me? How I'ma get what's mine?"

"You da c/o sweetheart dats on you to figure out."

"Oh I'll figure it out," she says and walks off.

I watch her go back to the desk then I look down at Joe who is sitting by himself. I really didn't wanna smack him but I knew that I had to set precedence. I wasn't really known throughout the city which meant that I was susceptible to a nigga trying me and because Joe had stepped out of line I had to make an example out of him. I did it to let niggas know that I wasn't for the bullshit. Setting an example was something that Tone had taught me and his teaching me that would be the cause of me catching my first homicide.

* * * * *

FEBRUARY 1993

It's amazing how fast the tides turn. It was two days after my birthday, I was fifteen and case working on the biggest strip in my hood. Me and Tone were in charge of the block and it was crazy. The day after my birthday Lefty was found murdered in his car on Hope Street. Word was he'd been shot twelve times.

All of a sudden Hancock was ripe for the taking. His workers were lost without Lefty and it could be seen that they didn't know what to do. They didn't even know where the work was so they could hustle. The entire day fiends came and went without being able to cop. Me and Tone reported this to Rosie but all she did was tell us not to worry about it because she had everything under control.

That night me and Tone sat on Rosie's steps and for the first time this major drug corner looked like a ghost town. Rosie came out and sat with us in the cold winter air and after a few minutes of meaningless conversation she pointed to the corner of the block.

"Tomorrow that becomes ours. Tomorrow we take back what is ours—what was my husband's. Tomorrow we take back Hancock and Cambria and can't nobody stop us."

We listened to what she was saying but in my heart I had my doubts. All Rosie had was me and Tone while there were a few other crews who had more people and could realistically take the corner if they wanted to but I kept my reservations to myself.

"I have sent messages to all of Lefty's workers and I told them that if they wanted to keep making money then they should come to the corner tomorrow morning. Tomorrow when they show up Pooh you will do the talking."

"Me?" I asked surprised that she would want me to have that responsibility especially when most of Lefty's workers were older than me. I wasn't even sure that they would respect me.

"Yes you. I see leadership in you and I want you to be my voice. You will lay the rules out for them and you will tell them that breaking these rules will not be tolerated. If rules are broken then you and Tone will punish whoever breaks them."

"What if dey ain't tryin to hear what I'm sayin?"

Rosie looked at me for a minute then she looked at Tone so I did the same. Tone was silent for a second then he looked me in the eye.

"They'll listen cause we'll make them."

"How?"

"We'll talk about dat later. Right now let Rosie finish," he said and I looked back to Rosie.

"You two will be the case workers. We will need another one but that will be a decision you will have to make. You and Tone will hire him whoever he is."

"Anything else?" I asked.

"Yes tomorrow someone will show up to hustle on the block. He'll be a moreno. Don't ask him any questions and let him do whatever he wants as long as he don't interfere with what we are doing."

"We goin let da competition sell on our corner?"

"He won't be any competition. He'll be selling crack. We

sell heroin," Rosie said and stood up off the steps.

"Anthony yebate al chamaquito y hablale, necesito que todo salga bien manana asegurate que lo mate," Rosie said to Tone in Spanish before entering the house.

"What did she say?" I asked Tone once she had closed the door.

"If you wanna know what's bein said around you in dis neighborhood you should learn to speak Spanish," Tone told me.

I looked at him but he said nothing more. He motioned for me to follow him to the car which I did. He got into the driver's side and I climbed into the passengers side and we pulled off. Years later I would find out that Rosie through Tone had ordered me to murder someone.

Me and Tone were sitting in the car on Water Street and since we had gotten there we hadn't spoken a word to one another. This wasn't unusual because Tone was a real quiet kind of guy. I looked out my window and wondered what could be our purpose for being there. What I wondered about more than that was how I was suppose to get a bunch of niggas that were older than me and probably didn't respect me to abide by some rules that I laid out. On top of that I didn't even know what the rules were.

"Tone is dis shit goin work tomorrow?"

"It'll work."

"I don't know. Yo I don't think dem niggas goin listen to me."

"You know why dem niggas goin listen?"

"Why?" I asked.

"Cause we goin make em."

"How we goin do dat?" I asked and instead of a verbal response all I got was a gun handed to me.

"I got a gun," I told him.

"I know dis for somethin else."

"What?"

"Tomorrow when we approach deez workers and you start talkin you gotta have something to catch dey attention. You gotta let em know dat we for real. One of our first rules is no heat on da corner and dat means no dumb shit like fuckin da fiends up."

Immediately I wondered where he was going with this. He was getting at something but I didn't know exactly what.

"An example has to be made and you have to be the one to do it. My aunt loves you and she has a lot at stake by putting you in the position that she is. She needs to be sure that you can handle what she is giving you and if I'ma be there with you den I need to be sure too."

"What you sayin Tone?"

"I'm sayin dat when da nigga dat kicked ya mom on da corner da otha day shows up you goin get out dis car and kill him."

"What?"

"You heard me. Dis is how we set our example. Dis is how you get your revenge and most of all dis is how you make sure dat da workers follow da rules dat you set for em."

"I ain't neva killed nobody before Tone."

"Don't worry it's easy just point and shoot." That was the second time that someone had told me that. The first being when Spud had killed Cuba's murderer. I fondled the gun in my hands then looked over to Tone who looked straight ahead. My hand trembled slightly then Tone tapped me and pointed to a figure coming up the street.

"If dis is him get out da car as soon as he get to da front bumper. No words, when you kill someone neva talk to em. It give em a chance to try somethin stupid. Point and squeeze. You eva shot a gun before?"

"No," I answered truthfully.

"Den aim for da body. It's a bigger target. When he falls from da body you shoot him in da head. Always make sure da job is finished."

As the walking individual got closer I grabbed the handle of the door but it wasn't the nigga we were looking for and I settled back into the seat. We waited for another ten minutes before another figure came walking towards us. This time it was my intended target. My heart began to beat real fast, my palms got moist and I suddenly felt queasy.

I knew that it was now or never. Everything Rosie had done for me was leading up to this moment and it was either do what was being asked of me or go back to being broke. I have to admit that I was scared to death and my shaking hand was evidence of that but I also knew that I wasn't going back to where I had come from so when he got close enough I opened the car door and got out with the gun in my hand. The guy I was going to kill wasn't even paying me any attention. I stepped forward into his path and he finally looked up. His face was battered from the stomping that I had given him and that made me feel good. I locked eyes with him for a minute then raised the gun and shot him square in the chest.

He fell back onto his ass then put his hand up to the wound and looked up at me. I recalled the day that this man had stomped my mother and with no hesitation I raised the gun and shot him in his head. His body flung backward and he lay motionless. I stood there looking at the body and probably would have continued to, had Tone not gotten my attention and told me to get in the car.

I jumped back into the passengers seat and Tone pulled off casually as if nothing had happened. He gave me a rag and told me to wipe the gun off which I did. Then we drove to the Delaware River where I tossed the gun into the river. We drove back to Rosie's in silence and when we finally stopped and parked Tone looked at me and noticed that my hand was shaking.

"Don't worry. It was ya first time. It gets easier. Tomorrow when you talk they will listen," he told me.

For the next two hours me and Tone sat in the car and during this time he told me what all the rules were and what the punishments would be for breaking them and continued to drill it into my head until I had it down pat. He also schooled me on what to say when I was addressing the workers.

When we were done I got out of the car and told Tone that I would see him in the morning. He told me to make sure that I was on time and I said that I would be and hopped into my car and pulled off. I drove to Kensington and Lehigh and got out, to use the payphone. I dialed a number and even though it was nearly two in the morning someone answered on the third ring. I talked to Lisette for a few minutes and when I was done she told me to come to her house. She said that she would be waiting on the porch for me.

* * * * *

That night was amazing. I went to Lisette's house just wanting to be in the company of another person because I was a nervous wreck after killing the nigga who had stomped my mom but it turned out to be much more. When I arrived she led me to her room and before I knew it I was having sex with the girl of my dreams.

I wasn't as experienced as I would have liked to have been but it was the most amazing moment of my young life. We fucked three times that night and after that we just laid in her bed talking to one another. After the talking I knew that this was the girl I wanted to be with forever.

Feeling self-conscious about my performance I asked Lisette had I satisfied her and she said that it didn't matter. She said that with time I would know how to please her like no man ever would. Then she told me that she was fully satisfied just being with me.

That night I told her about what I was going to embark upon the following day and all she did was tell me to be careful. She didn't try to tell me not to do it or anything like that. She told me that she was my girl and that she was going to support me in any way possible. We never did go to sleep that night and when the sun rose and her family began to wake she took me downstairs and introduced me to her mother and father and when she did she labeled me her boyfriend.

To my surprise her mother and father were pleased to meet me and treated me like family from the jump. Her mom sat me down at the kitchen table and made me breakfast and fussed over me while I ate. Her father didn't say much other than warning me that I had better take care of his baby girl. I also met her brothers and sisters and everyone took to me immediately. The age difference didn't matter to anyone. All that mattered to them was that Lisette was happy.

When it was time for me to go we stood on the porch and kissed and I told her that I wouldn't be able to pick her up from school. She said that she was cool but made me promise to call her when I got the chance and I promised. After a final kiss I hopped in my car and headed for my corner.

* * * * *

When I got to the corner Tone and the workers were waiting for me. I lit a cigarette before I got out of the car trying to calm my nerves then got out hoping that no one would notice my nervousness. I approached the crowd and shook Tone's hand then he nodded towards the workers and I took a deep breath. I had always been articulate and able to speak so I took another puff of the cigarette and went for what I knew.

"Y'all all here for one reason and dats to make money and dats what we goin do. Lefty gone. My Aunt Rosie own da corner now and anybody dat got a problem wit dat should step now. I don't know most of y'all. My name Pooh and from now on y'all report to me or my cousin Tone. I'ma lay da rules out for y'all and deez is da rule dat y'all goin follow or go somewhere else to hustle. Number one, no drawing attention to da corner. Y'all was doin a lot of dumb shit before. I came out here one time and had to fight one of y'all over a fiend he was fuckin wit. As you can see dat nigga ain't here dis morning. Dat type shit is done on dis corner."

I delivered the news just as Tone had told me to. He told me that by saying what I had about the nigga that I had killed that it would let them niggas know that I had done it without actually admitting to it. It was the perfect way to ensure that they would follow rules that I set forth. Over the next half hour I laid out the rules for them and all of the punishments that coincided with breaking them and when it was all over everyone was ready to go to work. Me and Tone went to Rosie's house and she told us where to pick up the work and two days after my birthday I was a caseworker on the biggest corner in my hood.

Chapter 5

OCTOBER 2000

C.F.C.F UNIT C2-1

I'm sitting in the dayroom watching TV when I hear the male guard on duty call my name. I walk to the desk and he tells me that I am wanted in the school building. Immediately my antennas go up. I don't attend school or any religious services so there is no reason for me to be going to the school building. The only plausible explanation that I can come up with is that I am being set up.

I have never been one to run from anything so I rack my brain trying to figure out what to do. Black, a dude from West Philly whom I have recently began speaking with on a daily basis walks past me and a plan formulates in my head.

I tell Black to come to my cell and he does without asking any questions. When we get to my cell I tell him what the c/o said and I tell him about my reservations. I ask him if he has a knife that I can use. Again without saying anything Black walks out of my cell and comes back a few minutes later with a banga and I thank him.

I tuck the knife on my waist, go back to the desk and get my pass from the guard then walk off the block heading for the Ed building. The whole way there I try to figure out who could have summoned me but I come up blank. Then it hits me.

I flash back to the two niggas that I trashed on quarantine and I can feel it in my gut that it's them. When I get to the Ed building a short, fat but slightly attractive female c/o is sitting at the desk and she takes my pass. She looks at my pass then tells me to go to the last room at the end of the hall. I look down the hallway then take a deep breath and start walking.

On my way I reach my hand under my shirt and grasp the handle of the homemade knife ready and prepared to do whatever needs to be done when I enter the room. I'm about twenty feet from the room when I notice the fat c/o chick watching me with a weird look on her face confirming my thoughts for me. Someone had set me up and she had played an intricate part in it.

I finally get to the door, I grab the handle and swing it open. To my surprise it's not a nigga or niggas waiting for me it's the same c/o chick that has been hassling me since I came through. I look back at the fat chick again and she gives me a smile and a head nod as I enter the room.

"What's up shorty?" I ask as I enter.

"My name is Michelle but you can call me Mi-Mi. Here," she says and tosses a zip-lock bag that had been compressed and taped up onto the table where she is sitting.

I pick up the package and just from the looks of it I can tell that there is a lot of weed in it and it shocks me that she actually did what I told her to do. It was only the day before when I gave her Rosie's address and told her to go get something for me. Truthfully I didn't think that she would. I thought she was bluffing but obviously she wasn't. I put the package in my back pocket then look at her.

"Good lookin."

"Good lookin my ass. I did what you asked now you gotta give me what I want."

Already knowing what she is talking about I pull my flaccid dick out of my pants and Mi-Mi gets right down on her knees and begins sucking until I grow to my full length which ain't as large as people would expect me to say. I mean I ain't got no baby dick or nothing like that but I don't lie on my dick either. I got enough to get the job done and Mi-Mi don't seem to have any complaints.

For about three minutes she sucks with a fury then out of the blue she stops. This really pisses me off because my eyes are just beginning to roll back into my head which means I'm close to cuming. She stands up and I look at her like she is crazy.

"What you do yo?" I ask her.

"I know you don't think I went through all dis trouble to come down here and suck some dick. Nigga you gotta fuck me."

"We ain't got time for all dat."

"My girl workin da desk. She ain't goin let us get caught," she tells me while undoing her belt and the button on her pants.

I can tell that she ain't goin let me get out of this and truthfully I don't mind. Realistically what man would turn down something like this. She pulls her black c/o pants down to her ankles and bends over the table she had been sitting at and I admire the beautifully shaped caramel brown ass that beckons me. I take the knife off of my waist and put it on the table then grab my dick with one hand while I use the other to spread her ass cheeks as best I can. She reaches in between her legs and spreads her pussy lips for me and I slide my dick in without too much trouble.

As soon as I am in she removes her hand and puts it back on the table to brace herself. I begin to pound away at the wet pussy and fat ass cheeks with all my might. If anybody were to walk by this room we would be caught because I'm pounding so hard that the sound of flesh hitting flesh is clearly audible.

Then to top it all off she begins to moan a little too loudly.

Knowing that she is making too much noise I pull off my blue shirt and tell her to bite down on it which she does. She moves her hips and grinds her ass back into me. Her doing this, combined with the great few minutes of dick suck that I received prior to us fucking has me ready to cum but I hold back because after all I do want to make a good first impression. I close my eyes, grab her hips and pound as hard as I can. She muffles moans through my blue shirt which is becoming stained with her saliva and that does it.

I can't take it no more and I pick my pace up. I'm sure she senses what is coming because she too picks up her pace and slides her hand back between her legs starting to play with her clit. I pump hard and fast for about another minute then just when I'm about to cum I pull out and shoot my skeet on her ass cheeks. After I cum I go soft and she continues to stimulate herself until she finally shudders and nearly collapses onto the table.

I stuff my dick back into my pants without wiping it off and she stands up straight turning to face me. She takes my shirt out of her mouth and hands it to me with her face wrinkled up.

"Why you pull out? I wanted to feel you cum in me."

"I don't need no more babies."

"I'm on da pill."

My face remains impassive but inside I'm thinking to myself 'yeah right'. I don't know who she thinks she talking to but I know how devious bitches can be and it'd be just my luck that I get her pregnant and then she tries to blackmail me. I can see it clearly. She pops up pregnant then threatens to tell Lisette or worse she keeps the baby and tries to juice me forever. No dice. I ain't no fool and that's something she better learn real quick.

"I feel you sayin you on da pill but I ain't takin dat risk."

"Whateva," she says as she's pulling her pants up and getting herself together.

"If you say so."

"You need anything else?"

"Na not right now, I'm cool," I tell her not wanting to burn her out.

"Here take dis," she says and pulls out a piece of paper with a phone number on it. "Dats my cell. Send it to ya peoples and wheneva you need something tell her to get wit me."

I put the number in my pocket and the knife back on my waist. I get ready to go out of the room but she stops me before I can open the door.

"Dis goin be our thing from now on so when dey call church on dis day make sure you come. My girl work down here so we can always use this room whenever we want. When you go out of da room wait for me at da desk and I'll walk through da hallway with you so you don't get searched on ya way back to da unit. Oh, and don't let me catch you with none of deez otha bitches all up in ya face. I'm all you need, trust me."

I shake my head as I walk out of the room and to the desk where I wait for a few minutes before she shows up. The fat chick signs my pass and me and Mi-Mi walk through the hallway together with enough space between us so as not to draw any suspicious glances. When I get to C-building she keeps going to D building and I get on the elevator that will take me to my floor.

Once I am back on the block I immediately go to the shower to wash mine and her juices off then I go to the phone to call Lisette. After talking to my wife and kids I summons Black and tell him to come to my cell. When he gets there I give him his knife and a nice amount of weed. He doesn't ask any questions. He just says good looking and goes on about his business. When he leaves I roll me a stick and use the electrical socket to light it and savor the great weed that Rosie has sent me.

When I'm done I sit back on my bed enjoying my high while replaying the session with Mi-Mi. I laugh to myself at her telling me that she wanted me to cum in her. I got three babies already and I surely don't want anymore unless it's with Lisette. Truthfully, I don't want anymore with Lisette but I wouldn't complain about it. My kids weren't planned pregnancies but shit happens.

* * * * *

MARCH 1993

Two months into running the corner and things couldn't have been better. The block was running smooth, the workers were listening and most importantly so far I hadn't had any hassle from the Homicide Detectives. There were rumors floating around that I had killed the nigga on Water Street but no one had come to lock me up so I wasn't worried.

This day I arrived on the block before all the workers just like always and went to Rosie's for breakfast. I sat at her table and ate while she talked business with me then I headed for the corner. I gave the workers their bundles and the day started. Fiends came from all over for the dope that Rosie was supplying and most of them didn't even leave the block before shooting up. Some just found a set of steps fixed and shot their death. I sat on my usual perch making sure that my spot ran smoothly. Then I noticed the four niggas getting out of the car.

Teddy, Miz, Boo and some nigga that I had never seen before all got out of a green car and stood around looking at all the traffic for a few seconds. After they were done scanning the block, Teddy's eyes came to rest on me and the trio walked towards me. I stood up off of the steps and waited for them to arrive.

"Pooh right?" Teddy asked when he walked up.

"Yeah."

"Dis my youngin Pudge," Teddy said introducing me to the nigga that I had never seen before. "He goin be out here doin his thing. I know Rosie already told you bout dis right?"

"Yeah she told me."

"Cool. My youngin know his place and he know what he pose to do so he goin make sure he stay out ya way aiight?"

"Cool wit me," I said as if I had a choice.

"Aiight we out," Teddy told me. Then him, Miz and Boo turned and walked back to their car, got in and drove off.

The nigga who I now knew to be Pudge said nothing when Teddy was gone. He simply went to the corner, found him a post and started to advertise the crack he would be slinging. I was actually surprised to see Teddy that morning. Rosie had told us that someone would be hustling on the corner but that had been two months ago and no one had ever shown up so I thought that it wasn't going to happen. It obviously was because Pudge was on our corner slinging Teddy's work.

Seeing this made me wonder why it was going on. I wondered why Rosie had agreed to let one of Teddy's workers post up on our block so I reminded myself to ask her when I had a chance. I sat back down on my steps and for the next four hours I watched the corner and scurried back and forth replenishing the workers with dope as they ran out. Around twelve in the afternoon I was coming out of Santos' store when I noticed a champagne-colored Honda Accord pull up on the corner. I immediately knew who was behind the wheel.

I had purchased the car two weeks prior. It was the first big thing that I had purchased with my new found cash flow. I knew that it was my car because it had a stuffed pit-bull in the rear window that Lisette had given me when I first got the car not to mention that she was driving. I watched her get out and just like she always did she turned heads as she walked by.

At 5'1" and 112 pounds Lisette was a small but extravagant package. Her titties were the perfect size for her body and her ass which wouldn't be considered fat compared to the asses of today was magnificent back then for a Puerto Rican girl. Her body was nice but it was her beauty that captured the attention of the male species. Sometimes beauty can't be explained. Sometimes it's just something you gotta see and this is one of those cases. You'll just have to take my word for it. If you've been paying attention to the shit that I've been saying you'll know I'm not the type to lie.

Lisette waited for a car to pass then crossed the street and walked into my arms and kissed me. I loved being with her. She had a way of making me feel like I was the most important and special man in the world and she did it in a way that I could tell that she was sincere. For the past month I had been practically living with Lisette and her family. I still went home everyday to check on my mom and give her money but at night I shared a bed with my girl.

As of lately I had been letting Lisette drive my car to school after she dropped me off on the block. I didn't mind because when I got to the block I seldom left unless I absolutely had to and if there was an emergency I could always use one of Rosie's cars. I actually had given my CRX to Lisette but it was in the shop at the time. I know a lot of people would call me a sucker for love but I didn't care. This day was a surprise. She had been to the corner at this time before but that was a one time thing. I didn't know what made her come that afternoon but I was about to find out.

"What's up?" I asked her when we finished kissing.

"I wanted to see you so I left school early."

"You ain't goin get in trouble?"

"Nope."

"Cool. You want somethin from the store?"

"Yeah get me a soda," she said and I went in and got her a Pepsi, her favorite soda.

We walked back to my steps and sat talking until I had to run to get some more dope for one of the workers. When I came back Tone was sitting with Lisette and they seemed to be deep in conversation. When I walked up I could hear Tone telling her to tell her girlfriend from Bottoms Up to get with him. She said that she would, then Tone got up and headed for Rosie's. When he left, Lisette got real quiet and for some reason when she spoke she wouldn't look me in my face like she normally did.

"Pooh I gotta tell you somethin."

"What's up?"

"Promise you won't get mad?"

"Why would I get mad?" I asked wondering where she was getting ready to go with this.

"I ain't neva tell you dis but I love you," she said and I began to have a bad feeling about what she was going to say.

"Yo say what you gotta say," I said pulling away from her.

"Why you move?" she asked.

"What you gotta tell me?"

She must have sensed what I was thinking because she pulled me back to her.

"It ain't nothin like dat asshole. I'm not cheatin on you.

I'm pregnant," she said and I froze.

I looked at her unsure of what to say. A million thoughts ran through my head all at the same time. The first was what was I going to do with a baby? The second was was it mine? My mom had always warned me about how treacherous women could be and recently Rosie had been warning me about what girls would do to get close to me because I was getting money.

"Papi I know you young and maybe not ready for dis so if you want me to I'll get an abortion but this is our baby and I really wanna have it but whateva you want to do I'll do it."

The moment those words left her lips I knew that the baby was mine. Don't ask me how I knew but I did. I knew that the baby was mine and that this was the woman for me. There was no way that I was going to tell her to have an abortion. She was right this was our baby and the beginning of our family.

"We goin have it," I said, my voice slightly wavering.

"You sure?"

"Yeah, I'm sure."

"Ooh baby I'll get a blood test whateva you want."

"You ain't gotta do none of dat."

"Pooh, I love you."

"I know you told me," I said as she jumped into my lap and kissed me deeply.

"Tonight you gotta come to my house early so we can tell my parents."

"You think dey goin be mad?"

"No dey love you."

"I hope so."

"Dey do, trust me."

"I don't know nothin bout raisin no baby," I told her.

"Don't worry we'll be aiight."

"If you say so."

"Don't you trust me?"

"Yeah."

"Den don't worry we'll be aiight."

"Okay."

"And don't be actin all insecure and shit either. I told you in the beginning I'm wit you. I'm da bitch. Let me be insecure."

"What you got to be insecure bout?"

"Please a young boy dat look like you and got some money I got a lot to be insecure about."

"No you don't."

"You sure?"

"Yeah, I got what I want on my lap," I said and we kissed again and I knew that I was in love.

Lisette had me open and at the time I didn't know it but I had her open too. We loved each other and we had a baby on the way. In my mind things couldn't get much better but they would. Not only would things get better but they would get worse too.

OCTOBER 2000

C.F.C.F UNIT C2-1

Just thinking about the beauty of Lisette makes my dick get hard even after all these years but for some reason I find myself comparing her beauty to that of Mi-Mi or c/o Michelle Ross. I've been thinking about her ever since yesterday when we fucked in the school building. Mi-Mi has a caramel brown complexion with a set of hazel brown eyes that seem to look into your soul when she engages you. Her body is ridiculous even in her uniform. Her ass is fat and her titties strain against the shirt she wears causing most of the men that she comes across to look at her chest before they look in her face. But please don't get it twisted. She can't compare to my Lisette in no way because I won't allow her to.

Mi-Mi is a bad bitch no doubt about it and I knew it the first time that we encountered each other. With Lisette it's something different. I'm in love with her and have been for seven years. To me she is the most beautiful woman in the world. You could line up the ten baddest bitches in the world and I would still take my Lisette over any one of them any day. But like I said I'm in love.

Now please understand this. I'm fallible just like any other man and me being the guy that I was on the streets I had plenty of encounters with females that weren't Lisette. Most of these were nothing more than fuck sessions and quick dick sucks. There were instances where I had a chick on the side but like Rosie taught me those came with the territory. None of those other woman mattered because they weren't Lisette. This is the category that Mi-Mi falls into.

I'm in jail and right now she is the means to an end and nothing more. Of course I would never tell her this but if it ever came a time when she couldn't serve a purpose for me anymore then she would become as irrelevant to me as an 8-track tape. For now though I'll let her believe whatever she wants to as long as she does what I say.

I look out my cell door to check on the c/o and after noticing that he is chilling at the desk I spark up a joint. This weed is the shit even Black thought so. He must have shared it with someone because he came to my cell earlier and said that his man was fucked up off of it. He asked me if I had any for sell and I told him that I would have to get back to him later. I like Black but I don't know how much yet. He a cool dude with that natural flyness that most West Philly dudes possess but that don't mean that I trust him so I'm still on the cusp of what I should do. I only gave him the weed last night because he let me hold his knife with no questions asked. While I'm not sure what to do and what not to do with him yet I do know that there is a lot of money to be made on this block and in this jail and I plan on making it. I need to get my feet wet first but when I get the hang of things I'm going to have Rosie and Mi-Mi flood this joint.

I'm a hustla through and through thanks to Rosie and it's all I know how to do now. When I see an opportunity I try to take advantage of it and this is definitely an opportunity to make some nice money but like I said I got to get my feet wet first before I jump into the deep end of the pool. Make no mistake about it though, sooner or later I will go swimming.

Chapter 6

NOVEMBER 2000

C.F.C.F UNIT C2-1

"Yo Black said somebody wanna cop some tree," my celly says as he enters the cell.

"I ain't got none for sell right now. All I got is enough for us. Tell Black to tell whoeva it is dat he goin have to wait," I tell my celly and he goes back out the cell.

I like my celly. He's a good dude. We been living together for about a month now and it's been alright all things considered. His name is Cory and he from West Oak Lane. He locked up for a body but you would never be able to tell. I've never seen him stress and he always has a smile on his face. When he first moved into the cell he did a little too much talking but now I put up with his rambling because it's his only fault. He doesn't draw heat to me or what I'm doing and he is actually quite useful in this regard. He's clean and he doesn't depend on me to support him which is all I can ask for given my current predicament.

I'm done getting my feet wet and I'm officially in the deep end of the pool. It's a lot of money to be made in the jail and since I have the means I may as well utilize them. Mi-Mi brings in whatever I ask without question and she does it whenever I ask. I've been using Black as my middle man mainly because I don't want too many people in my business. Most people think that it's him that's making the moves and I have no problem with that because it's one less hassle that I have to worry about.

I'm currently waiting for Mi-Mi to bring me some more weed and some pills which is the big thing for these niggas. A lot of them love to pop pills and since that is where the money is I had Rosie get me 200 pills which she gave to Mi-Mi. I should get the package tonight. Also I'm about to get a cell phone because the phone time that I get from the jail just don't do it for me. I still got money on the streets and I need to make certain calls to make sure that all of my affairs are in order. Plus I got a chick out of state that I need to talk to but can't because Lisette gets all of my phone time. I'ma tell Mi-Mi to get me a phone.

My celly comes back and when he does Black is with him. I look up as they enter the cell and shut the door behind them. I still don't fully trust Black and because of this I keep him on a short leash and tell him only what he needs to know.

"Pooh my man wanna holla at you," Black tells me.

"For what?"

"He wanna talk business."

"What he wanna talk business wit me for. Why he ain't talkin to you?"

"He said he wanna talk to da main man." "How he know I'm da main man?"

"He don't. He just know dat I ain't."

"Yeah well either he talk to you or he don't talk at all. I don't talk to no niggas I don't know."

"He say he wanna spend some money."

"So tell him to tell you what he wanna do."

"He ain't goin tell me. I already tried."

"Well den he don't wanna do no business. I need to holla at my celly for a minute. I'll get wit you later," I say letting Black know that it is time for him to exit the cell which he does.

When he leaves I stand at the door and watch where he goes. He walks over to a nigga named Tariq who is known throughout the jail as a ryda. He stabbed a few niggas and his reputation preceded him all over the jail. I watch Black say something to him then I watch Tariq look up to my cell. We lock eyes for a minute then he looks away and walks to his cell.

"What you know bout da nigga Riq?" I ask my celly.

"Nothin but what I heard."

"What's up wit him and Black?"

"I guess dey aiight. Dey used to be together when we was on D-side."

"Get da banga out da mattress," I tell him.

"Why?"

"Cause I'ma need it."

* * * * *

Tonight, soon as the evening count is cleared I'm called for an official visit. During this visit with my lawyer absolutely nothing new is revealed. He updates me on certain aspects of the investigation he is doing and even though neither one of us want to say it we know that it is useless. We both know that he is being paid simply to do everything he can to stop me from being legally executed by the state. The visit lasts like 45 minutes then I head back to the block.

The rest of the inmates have been let out by the time that I get back and I spot my celly waiting in the phone line. I walk over to him and ask him if the guard has called my name and he says no. I figure that Mi-Mi hasn't been on her lunch break yet and decide to wait in the dayroom for a little while to see if I get called or not.

I sit in front of one of the TV's not really paying attention to the program that is airing when Tariq walks over and sits next to me.

"What's up Pooh?"

"Chillin."

"Yo I need to holla at you bout somethin." "What?"

"I'm tryin to cop some weed."

"I ain't got none."

"Dats not what I hear."

"You heard wrong."

"Look I dig dat you tryin to stay unda da radar. I'm just tryin to get high. I got money to spend."

"Dats what's up but I ain't got no weed."

"Why you actin like a nut?" he asks and I can tell that he is becoming impatient which I don't give a fuck about.

"What you mean actin like a nut?" I ask.

"I mean come on dog it's only a little weed."

"I feel what you sayin' but I told you I ain't got none."

"What's up?" Black asks as he approaches me and Riq.

"Nothin man. Dis is why you can't let deez nut ass niggas get nothin cause dey act like dey bosses."

"What da fuck is you tryin to say Riq? You ain't gotta shoot no indirect shit if you got somethin you wanna get off ya chest. Say it nigga man da fuck up.

"If I had somethin to say nigga I'd say it," he tells me.

"Whateva," I say and get up and walk to my cell.

When I get to my cell I place my knife on my waist and wait for what I know is going to happen. It is inevitable. Riq is used to niggas bending for him but that's not me. I don't bend for nobody. I stick to my guns and a niggas rep can't change that. A nigga gotta prove to me that he earned his rep and that's exactly what Riq was goin have to do. Truthfully this could have been avoided if I would have just sold him the weed but I just couldn't. I don't do business on the streets with niggas I don't know so why would I come to jail and start. I can't. It's just not my style plus I don't want the nigga thinking that he put the pressure on me.

I stand in my door and watch Riq and his movements and eventually he starts to ascend the steps to the top tier. Black is trailing behind him and this shows me, that I was right not to trust him. I step back from my cell door and keep my hand on my knife. When they get to my cell Riq grabs the handle of the door and pulls it open. He peeks in and seeing me near the back of the cell comes in.

"Where dat shit at my man?" he asks entering and pulling his knife out.

"I told you I ain't got nothin," I tell him while watching Black come through the door. He's such a coward that he can't even look me in my eye.

"Don't make me bang you out dog just give me da weed. My man already told me dat you got some in here so just give me dat shit."

"Whatevea I got in here you goin have to take."

Riq is so used to niggas folding under his pressure that he doesn't even notice that my hand is under my shirt the whole time. He advances towards me and grabs me by my shirt. The next thing he does is reach for my back pocket and as soon as he does I stick him in his stomach. He immediately lets me go and backs up.

The sight of his own blood must have flipped a switch on inside of him because instead of backing out of the cell like I thought he would he charges me. The next thing I know we're struggling with each other trying to avoid getting stabbed.

As soon as we start Black runs out of the cell. Riq who is stronger than me gets his knife hand free and stabs me in my shoulder and in my side. The pain ain't as bad as I thought it would be or maybe it's just the adrenalin pumping through my veins. I quickly find his knife hand again and grasp it and we begin tussling again banging into the walls, the toilet and anything else that gets in our way.

I punch him in his face twice and he slips in a good punch to my jaw once again freeing up his knife hand. He stabs me in my forearm because I lift it just in time to block the blow that would have most likely lodged the knife in my chest. The knife actually gets stuck in my forearm and Riq panics. He lets my knife hand go to try and get his knife out of my arm and I seize the moment. I bring my knife up swiftly and stab him in his jaw and neck.

I just knew that it was over when this happened but to my surprise Riq acts as if I haven't just stabbed him twice. He lifts me up off of my feet and slams me to the ground hard. I land on my back and the impact knocks the wind out of me. I lose my bearings and Riq finally gets the knife out of my arm. At this moment I see my life flash before my eyes because I see him bring his knife up past his shoulder and I know that he intends to plunge it into me and I can't mount a defense because I am dazed from the slam.

Somebody was definitely praying for me because out of the blue the cell door opens and in rushes my celly. As soon as he sees what is going on he tackles Riq off of me and they begin to wrestle for the knife. It takes me a few seconds to get my bearings but as soon as I do I jump up and now we have Riq on the ground and we stomp him. I realize that I still have my knife in my hand but there is no way that I want a jailhouse homicide so I just continue to stomp and kick him until a flock of c/o's rush the cell.

My celly had left the door open when he had came in and the c/o working could see what was going on from the desk. I guess he called for help. They rushed me and Cory and after a brief struggle they subdue and handcuff us then call for a nurse to come to the block and check Riq out.

One of the guards notices that I am stabbed too and they start to ask me what happened. I say nothing. I am beginning to feel woozy and when I look at the knife that Riq had I feel lucky because he surely could have killed me with what he had. The nurse arrives and they put Riq on a stretcher and make me walk to medical. Cory is taken straight to the hole and he says that he'll see me when I get there.

Once we get to medical I am taken into a room and one of the nurses examines me. She decides that my wounds aren't serious enough to warrant a trip to the outside hospital so she simply begins to stitch me up. Riq on the other hand is taken to a hospital because they fear he may have lost too much blood from the numerous wounds and the wound to the neck scares the nurses. They don't want him to die because they were negligent. I see them push him past my room and I decide that he definitely earned his rep.

My side and shoulder wounds have been stitched and the nurse is starting on my forearm when someone appears in the doorway of my room. I look up and standing there with her hands on her hips is Mi-Mi. She obviously knows the nurse and she asks her what's wrong with me. The nurse explains that I was stabbed but that I would be alright in a few days.

Mi-Mi says nothing to me but she gives me this look that says that she is masking her anger but at the same time concerned. I wink to let her know that I'm okay and she gives me a faint smile. She mouths to me that she'll see me tomorrow and walks away from the room.

While the nurse stitches my last wound I think about what happened and it amazes me that the nigga Riq thought that he could just rob me and get away with it. Even though I gave him his props by saying that he earned his rep doesn't mean that I would let him enhance it on me. Sitting on the table getting stitched up made me think about the time that I got shot. That night some niggas did take something from me and I let them but that would be the last time that ever happened.

* * * * *

MAY 1993

I had never imagined making so much money in my life.

The money came so fast that I didn't have time to spend it which was a good thing because I now had a stash. Rosie told me how important saving my money was and I was doing exactly that. Truthfully after buying my car and a bunch of clothes there was nothing else for me to really buy.

I gave my mom money whenever she asked which was every couple days. I gave Lisette money whenever she asked for it which was really only when she saw something that she wanted to buy for the baby. Other than that the only other things I really spent money on was to get high and food. Stashing money was a must now. I had a baby on the way.

I was really beginning to get excited about having a baby. I had told my mom but she was high and did nothing but utter some unintelligible response when I told her before nodding back off. I had written Spud and told him and he was happy for me. I had also sent him some pictures of me and Lisette together so he could see what she looked like and he totally approved. The members of the Puerto Rican side of my family were ecstatic when I told them that I was going to be a father and as always they were supportive.

Lisette's family was supportive too. They had done exactly what she had said they would do. They totally accepted her being pregnant by me and they were going crazy getting ready for the new arrival even though she was only three months pregnant. Lisette was probably the most excited. She had told all of her friends that she was pregnant by me and now everybody who knew us in Olney High School knew that we were about to have a baby.

Now that I was making some nice money, things were changing for me. I was becoming known in the neighborhood and people that previously walked by me without acknowledging me now made sure they spoke when they saw me. Females of all ages were beginning to stop and talk to me offering me all kinds of shit from dick sucks to quickies in alleyways. Older dudes from strips close by like Hope Street, Waterloo Street and Mutter Street were beginning to take notice of me and now they spoke when we came across each other.

While I enjoyed my new found celebrity Rosie warned me not to let it go to my head and to always be on point because you never could tell when shit could get crazy. Tone also began drilling helpful things into my head. By then we were closer than ever and I looked up to him. When it came to business I modeled the way that I did things after him. When it came to business he conducted himself with such force that anybody in his path had good reason to worry.

Tone was from Puerto Rico, La Perla to be exact. La Perla which meant The Pearl in English was notorious for the violence and drug dealing that went on inside of its walls. Tone had been raised inside of those rough walls so he was ready for the streets of Philly when he arrived. From his experiences in his homeland he had taught me a lot about the streets and how to survive in them.

Tone was a stickler for doing things the right way. When he saw one of the workers slacking off or doing something wrong he corrected them immediately and the same went for me and even Rosie. In the short time that we had been together I had learned a lot from Tone and was grateful to have him by my side. He was truly dedicated to what he did. I rarely seen him doing anything leisurely. Almost everything he did was connected to the corner. The one time that I thought I had caught him doing something other than his norm proved to me how truly dedicated he was.

Mama was a Puerto Rican chick who at the time was about 21. She was well known around the hood for being one of the guys. It was a well known fact that she would rumble anybody male or female and there were even stories of her shooting a few people. For days she had been coming to the corner and sitting with Tone while he worked. I thought for sure that he was trying to fuck her. Mama wasn't beautiful but she wasn't ugly either. She was definitely fuckable. I watched this go on for a few days then one day I approached Tone while she was sitting with him and I told him to take the shift off and go chill with her. I told him that I would work his shift for him while he took care of his business.

The entire time that I'm saying this I have this sly smirk on my face as if to say to him. 'Yeah nigga I caught you' but Tone's face remains impassive as he looks at me for a minute then introduces Mama as our new caseworker. I look at him like he's joking but he doesn't smile. He tells me that the whole time that she's been coming to the corner he's been training her to take over the first shift.

They speak a few words to each other in Spanish then she gets up and walks away. When she leaves I sit next to him and he tells me how he seen her shoot someone a few weeks ago with no hesitation and how he was impressed with that. He said that she wouldn't be a pushover when it came to the workers and that she had experience from case working on another corner. He never asked me if I approved of him hiring her but I think he knew that if I didn't that I would have said something to him.

It was another lesson for me. It taught me to never think that I had anybody figured out without being positive of what was going on with that person or the situation that was playing itself out. That same day I would learn another lesson and I would learn it the hard way.

Later that night at about 10:00 P.M. I was working because Rosie had gone to meet with her connect and taken Tone with her. Tone had offered to stay with me but I told him that I had everything under control so he went with Rosie to secure her wellbeing. I was coming out of the stash house when a nigga whose name I didn't know but face I recognized, met me at the steps. Out of nowhere another nigga appeared and I knew this nigga too but like the first, only by face.

Before I could speak two guns were brandished and both were pointed at me. I looked at the niggas like they were crazy because they weren't wearing any masks and surely they knew that I would be able to tell Rosie and Tone who robbed me. At the time I wasn't street smart enough to know that niggas who didn't wear masks didn't care about anybody knowing that it was them because they plan to kill whoever they are victimizing.

The first one ordered me to give him everything I had and because Rosie had instructed me to never argue or try to fight with a robber I gave him the bundles that I had in my pocket. He asked for the money but I told him that I had already turned it in. Another thing that I learned from Rosie, never have the money and the product on you at the same time.

The one that I gave the bundles counted them and I guess he was satisfied because he put them in his pocket. I thought it was over but I was wrong. He fired his gun twice, both shots hitting me in my stomach sending me crashing to the pavement. As I curled up and grabbed my stomach I could feel the blood pouring from my wounds and at that instant I just knew that I was going to die.

Right then nothing mattered. Not the money I had made or my half-assed celebrity status. All I could think about was how young I was. I was fifteen years old and I was about to die. I was losing consciousness fast and right before I passed out I heard the voice of one of my workers yelling for someone to call an ambulance because I had been shot.

* * * * *

People say that you see a light when you about to die but that's bullshit because I was clinically dead for three minutes and I ain't see shit. I ain't see nothing until I woke up in the ICU of Temple Hospital. When I first woke up I didn't know where I was or what the fuck was going on. All I knew was that I felt like I was dead and that I had tubes coming out of every hole in my body except for my ass. A few minutes after I woke a doctor came to my bedside and explained my condition to me.

One of the shots that hit me went in and out but the other had done the damage. It had fucked up my large intestine and the bleeding inside of my body had been so uncontrollable that they had to cut me open and go in to fix it. A portion of my intestine had to be removed and it was during this procedure that I had died. Somehow after three minutes of working, the doctors had managed to get my heart beating again and finished the surgery.

The doctor told me that I had lost a lot of blood and that I was lucky to be alive. After all of the bad news he did give me some good news when he told me that I was finally out of the woods and that I should make a full recovery. He told me that my mom had been in the waiting room since the day that I came in and that he would bring her in in a minute. He checked my blood pressure and my heart then he told me that he was going to remove the tube from my throat. He told me to cough and as I did he pulled the tube. It felt as if I was going to throw up. A few seconds later the feeling subsided and he told me that he was going to go get my mom.

I was excited and happy to know that my mom had been there by my side during this whole ordeal. I began to think that maybe this experience would make her want to get her life back on track and give up the drugs but all of my thoughts were for nothing. When the doctor returned it wasn't my mom with him it was Rosie. The doctor led her to my bed and left us alone. The look on my face must have spoken volumes about how I was feeling because Rosie clarified the situation immediately.

"I only said I was your mom because they said only immediate family could come back here to see you."

"Where my mom at?"

"I don't know. Tone saw her on the corner and told her what happened but all she did was cop and leave."

Hearing this broke my heart. All the years that she had been a fiend my mom had always had my respect for one reason and that was because I knew that she loved me. Now the drugs had too firm of a grip on her. She had been told that her only son had been shot and she didn't even show up to the hospital to see if I was alive or not. A tear fell from my eye and Rosie wiped it away.

"I'm sorry baby I know it hurts."

"Did she know what hospital I was at?"

"Yeah. I went to your apartment the other day to try to get her to come but she wouldn't even answer me when I talked to her. It was like she was in another world."

"She didn't say nothin?"

"She asked me for some money for dope."

It was official my mom was in another world where I didn't exist. What really amazed me was that only a year ago she wasn't this far gone. This was her eleventh year as a dope fiend but when she was ten years deep she hadn't been in this deep a funk. It wouldn't be until years later that I understood how my mom had gotten so bad in just a years time. I would realize that it had been partly my fault. The year timeframe in which she took her turn for the worse would coincide with the year that I got into hustlin. It was during that year that I had supplied her with a lot of money and a lot of heroin. During that year she didn't have the past worries that she used to have. She didn't have to worry about where the next fix was going to come from. All she had to worry about was shooting the dope. It was during this year that my mom shot herself into the point of no return.

I lay there silently and Rosie respected the silence by doing nothing more then holding my hand. After a while I looked at her fully prepared to do what my mother had done to me. I was ready to forget about her. I know it sounds harsh and I know that most people could not even begin to understand how I could say or do such a thing. To some I probably sound like an asshole but before you judge me look at it from my perspective.

I'm fifteen years old and even though I was doing grown man things I was still a little boy, a little boy who needed his mother. The one person who was supposed to love me the most in the world was the one who had let me down the most. I was definitely ready to forget about her and I was ready to do it immediately.

"Where Tone?" I asked Rosie changing the subject.

"You know where he at."

"On da block."

"Of course. He sends his love."

"I know who robbed me."

"Don't worry about it."

"I don't know dey names but I know dey faces. I seen em before."

"Pooh don't worry about it."

"Why not?"

"Because it's over."

"What you mean it's over?"

"It's over. Tone took care of it."

When she said that I knew that nothing more needed to be said. If she said that Tone took care of it then I knew that the niggas that robbed me were no longer with us.

"How's Lisette?" I asked.

"Oh my god she is going crazy. I had to send her home a few days ago and tell her not to come back because she was making me crazy. That girl loves you Pooh. You better hold onto her."

"I will."

The doctor came back and told Rosie that I needed to rest. He told her that I would be moved to a regular room soon then she could visit all she wanted. She bent down and kissed me on the forehead and told me that she wasn't going anywhere and that she would be in the lobby and I thanked her. As I watched her leave I realized how lucky I was to have her in my corner. The doctor did a few more quick tests then left me alone with my thoughts.

Alone in the dark ICU with nothing but other critical patients and the humming and buzzing of hospital machines I did what I never thought I would be able to do. I kicked my mom out of my life. It infuriated me that she had not come to be by my side during my time of need. I had been shot and actually died and she never once showed her face to see if I was okay. I would be in the hospital for three weeks and never once would she come to see me.

Rosie and Tone came regularly. Lisette came everyday and her mom came a few times also. Rebecca came and all of my aunts and uncles on my Puerto Rican side showed up but never once did my mom and by the time I was released, in my mind I didn't have a mom.

CHAPTER 7

JANUARY 2001

C.F.C.F UNIT D2-1

Today is my first day back in population after doing sixty days in the hole. The hole wasn't as bad as I thought it would be. I mean it ain't nowhere you want to be but Mi-Mi made sure that my stay was as comfortable as possible. You can't survive on the small trays that they serve in population so in the hole where you can't have any commissary it's almost impossible to ever not be hungry.

Everyday like clockwork Mi-Mi would show up with food for me. She told me that her and the guard that worked the block were cool so he let her take care of me. When she said cool I didn't know if they were cool like homies or cool like he was fucking her but either way I ain't care. All that mattered to me was that I wasn't starving.

In the food which was always from the streets I would find cigarettes and weed and little notes wrapped in plastic and I knew that hooking up with her was the best move that I had made in a while. Tonight when she came to bring me my food she would be in for a surprise. There is no doubt in my mind though that as soon as she finds out that I'm out of the hole that it would only be a matter of time before I was called to the school building.

When I arrive on D2-1 it is three o'clock in the afternoon and the shifts have just changed. When I step on the block I notice that it is locked down which is the norm for a block with multi-purpose rooms. Blocks with these rooms have more people on them and in order for the block to be open there has to be two guards working. When I arrive there is one female guard there and she looks up at me as I walk onto the block.

"You Darnell Nevins?" she asks me.

"Yeah."

"You just got out the hole right?"

"Yeah."

"Come to the desk," she tells me as if I wasn't on my way there.

I walk to the desk and drop the plastic bags containing my belongings. She looks me up and down then snickers to herself. I wonder what the fuck is so funny so I ask her.

"Somethin funny?"

"You alright boo. My name Daniels, Mi-Mi told me to make sure you cool."

I looked at her skeptically wondering how she knows about me and Mi-Mi. I was under the impression that what we were doing was not something that she would want a lot of people knowing about. Daniels must see the look on my face because she tries to put me at ease.

"Don't worry. Mi-Mi is my girl. She called me a few minutes ago and told me that you were coming to the block. She wanted to make sure that you ain't have to go in a multi with all those other niggas."

"I ain't goin in a multi?"

"Na I got a cell for you."

This shocked me because it was a well known

fact that if you went to a block that had multis then that was where you went and waited your turn to get a cell. It shocked me that Mi-Mi had this much clout.

"You're going in seven cell. We locked down right now but you'll be out soon as the other guard gets here. It don't really matter because your celly is the laundry man so your door stay open anyway. If you need anything before I open the block come and let me know," she says and I nod my head.

I grab my bags and head to my cell. On my way there I see niggas in their doorways looking at me but I pay it no attention. When I get to my cell my celly is sitting on the bottom bunk eating cereal. He nods to me when I enter and I return the gesture then put my bags down.

"You just get out da hole?" he asks.

"Yeah."

"You got any laundry dat need to be washed?"

"Yeah I got a little."

"Get it ready and I'll get it later and wash it."

"Good lookin."

My celly gets up and washes his bowl out and exits the cell. I'm in the cell for about a half hour getting my shit together when he comes back in.

"Yo, my name Gee dog," he says and extends his hand which I accept and shake.

"Yo, dig dis. I don't like bein in nobody business but it's a couple niggas asking bout you," he tells me.

"Askin bout me for what?"

"I don't know dey wanted to know ya name and if you just came out da hole and shit like dat."

"What you tell em?"

"Nothin."

"Aiight good lookin."

"No problem. I don't know you but you my celly and I ain't want no niggas runnin up on you and you ain't on point."

"Yeah dats whats up."

A few minutes later the block opens and I come out of my cell with what my celly just told me heavy on my mind. I just got out of the hole and as soon as I step on the block niggas is asking about me. I know that it has something to do with the shit that happened with the nigga Tariq. While I was down the hole there was niggas talking about it and I could sense the aggressiveness in some of their voices.

I stand in front of my cell and look around the block looking at some of the faces moving about around me and I spot one that I recognize. It's one of the niggas that was all indirect on the door in the hole talking about how Tariq was his man and what he was going to do to the nigga that stabbed him. I know that he was only talking that shit because we was on different tiers and couldn't come out together. Nonetheless I know that I could be on my way back to the hole so I decide to get on the phone and talk to my wife and kids.

Surprisingly the phones are empty save for one person who's utilizing them. This is a rarity because these phones are usually always filled up. I grab a phone and call Lisette and we talk for my whole twenty-five minutes. It is great to hear her voice and the voices of my kids and as always this lifts my spirits. I tell her that I might be on my way back to the hole and she is pissed off at first but after I explain to her what is going on she fully understands. We share a few I love yous then I hang up.

I really love that girl. Since I been locked up she's never missed a visiting day. I get 6-8 letters from her a week and she has never missed one of my phone calls. She is truly my rock and I don't know what I would do without her.

When I hang up the phone I look towards my cell and notice three niggas standing in front of it. One of them is the same indirect nigga from the hole. I would really rather not have to go through this now but I don't know how to run from nothing so I walk in that direction. The niggas notice me coming and all turn in my direction. I ain't got no knife or nothing but fuck all that. I'ma always stand like a man. I'm about twenty feet from my cell when my name is called. I turn and look at the nigga who called me and when I see who it was I smile.

"Heem what's up?" I ask and walk towards my homie.

We hug when we reach one another then we begin asking each other a bunch of questions. I haven't seen Heem in over a year because he's been in here fighting a homicide. Heem is from the other side of Broad street the "High Numbers" and even though he's not from my hood we're good friends.

Our friendship stems from our business dealings with one another which were good for the both of us. Heem had a chick that lived on Hancock Street and through her he politicked until he found a nigga to sell him good quality work.

Lucy was a cool chick. We had known each other for a while at the time and she was like Rosie's little sister. When she first started bringing Heem around I watched him and how he conducted himself and I also watched who he did business with. Most of the time he ended up doing business with nobodies because all the niggas that had the means were skeptical of him. After about two months of watching him I approached him and offered him some of the blunt I was smoking. He accepted it knowing that it was a test and puffed on it inhaling and blowing the smoke back into my face. I asked him straight up if he was a cop and he told me that he wasn't. Then he lifted his shirt up to show me that he wasn't wearing a wire.

For some reason I trusted him. Maybe it was the way that he worked to get what he wanted. Maybe it was his whole demeanor. Whatever it was it had earned him a shot. I told him where to be and at what time and walked off never discussing price or quantity. He was at the designated place at the designated time and he was handed a bag by one of my workers who simply quoted him a number. A few days later he was back with that quoted number in money. He attempted to hand me the money but I refused it telling him that it wasn't mine. He caught my drift and searched for the worker that had given him the product. When he found him he walked over to him and handed him the money.

He talked to the worker for a minute then the worker signaled to me and I waited until he entered the stash house before going to meet him. When I got inside the worker told me that Heem said that he appreciated what I did but that he wasn't looking to work for nobody. The worker told me that Heem said that he wanted double what he had gotten if it was possible.

I hesitated when he said double and debated with myself on whether it was a worthwhile risk or not. I thought for a few minutes before quoting a price to my worker who nodded his head and went back outside. I watched the worker go to Heem and quote him the number I had given him. Heem nodded his head and the deal was done. Me and Heem did business like this for six months before I ever talked to him face to face but eventually we dealt with each other straight up and it was beneficial for the both of us and eventually the business blossomed into a good friendship.

"Damn Pooh what's up nigga? I seen ya ass on da news."

"Shit is crazy dog. What's up wit ya case?"

"I don't know dog, It could go either way." "Hopefully you come up off dat joint."

"Yeah hopefully. What bout you? How dat shit lookin?"

"You don't wanna know."

"Dat bad?"

"Worse."

"Dat's crazy."

"I know."

"Where you comin from?"

"Da hole."

"For what?"

"I banged da bul Tariq out."

"Yeah?"

"Yeah. He got me too but I got his ass worse."

"Yeah, I heard he got sent out but I ain't know it was ya work."

"Yeah, he tried to brody me."

"Dats definitely his thing. It's a few of his flunkies over here dem niggas suckas though." "You mean dem niggas in front of my hut?" "What hut you in?" he asks and I point to the cell with the three niggas in front of it.

"How you come right on da block and get a hut?" Heem asks.

"Long story," I respond.

"What you wanna do?" he asks in reference to the niggas in front of my cell.

"I don't give a fuck if dey wanna holla. We can do dat."

"Dis shit ain't bout nothin come on," he says and we walk to my cell.

"What's up?" Heem asks the indirect nigga as we approach.

"Ain't shit Heem. We just waitin to holla at poppy," he says referring to me.

"For what?" Heem asks.

"We just need to holla at him."

"All y'all?"

"Chill Heem. It ain't bout nothin."

"If it ain't bout nothin why it's three of y'all standin in front of my man cell?"

"I just told you we was waitin to holla at dude."

"Aiight let's go in da hut."

"What?" Indirect asks as if what Heem has said has caught him off guard. It is then that I realize that these three niggas is pussies.

"I said let's go in da hut. You said you wanted to holla at him so lets go in and holla."

"We wanna holla at him, not you."

"Dis my man so you goin have to holla at me one way or da other."

"Aye Heem." Indirect starts but Heem cuts him off.

"Shut up you fuckin nut y'all niggas actin like y'all goin move out on somebody. Yall niggas bitches runnin round here holdin Riq dick get da fuck outta here before I smack one of yall niggas." Obviously, they were exactly what I thought they were because they tuck their tails and walk away after being checked in front of basically the whole block. Then me and Heem go in my cell to catch up with one another.

* * * * *

Amazingly tonight the jail didn't do any recounts and we were let out of our cells on time. I come out and stretch and Heem walks up to me and shakes my hand.

"Yo, ain't nobody got no cigarettes over here? I need to smoke," I ask him.

"Man it's dry as shit over here right now. I had a horse but dude got caught up and dey fired him. Now I'm working through da visiting room and my chick."

"I got a horse. I'm just waitin for her to come through."

"Who ya horse?" Heem asks and I do something I never do. I tell somebody my business. I tell Heem because I know that I can trust him and because I want to see if he can give me any info on dis broad.

"Some chick named Ross."

"Get da fuck outta here."

"What?"

"C/o Ross with da fat ass?"

"Yeah why?"

"Nigga you ain't got dat stop lyin."

"When you eva known me to lie Heem?"

"Dog you know how many niggas in da jail and on da streets is tryin to lock dat down?"

"Naw I neva seen her till I got here."

"Dats cause you neva leave ya hood. Man niggas is tryin to do whateva dey can to get wit Shorty."

"What's up wit her?"

"She bad nigga. Dats what's up wit her."

"I know she bad nigga but what's up wit her? It seem like she do what she want round here."

"Her pop some type of big shot. I heard dat he in charge of all da county jails. I don't know da name of his position but dey say dat he da head nigga in charge."

"Is you serious?"

"Yeah dats what I heard."

"What she doin workin here?"

"My old horse said dat she work here cause da pay good and she can do whateva she want. She don't really do no work she just walk around and do what she want. Da only time she work is when dey short on guards and dey need her to."

"Dats why she walk around here like she own da joint?"

"Ain't no doubt. Who goin question da daughter of da nigga who run da whole operation?"

"I guess you right."

"You got her for real?" Heem asks still not believing what I was saying was the truth.

"Yeah dog I'm telling you."

Just as I was saying this, the door to the block opens and in walks the chick in question. Mi-Mi turns the head of every nigga on the block when she walks onto the unit. The lust in niggas eyes was unbelievable. If she had this effect in a c/o's uniform I can just imagine what it was like when she walked into a club in street clothes. She walks to the desk and says something to Daniels then hands her a brown paper bag. They talk for a few minutes then Daniels calls me over the intercom. I look up to the desk and Mi-Mi is waving me over to her. I walk to the desk and stand in front of it. Mi-Mi smiles upon my arrival. Daniels excuses herself and does a tour of the unit so we can talk.

"You aiight?" Mi-Mi asks when the c/o was gone.

"I'm cool. What about you?"

"I'm better now dat you out da hole."

"I'm glad to be out."

"What happened on C-block? Why you was trippin like dat?"

"Da nigga tried to take somethin from me dat ain't belong to him."

"You gotta chill. How we gonna do our thing if you all locked in da hole?"

"You already know how I get down, I ain't lettin no nut shit slide."

"I understand dat but from now on chill. Bein in da hole get corny after a while."

"You just want me out here so I can lay da pipe."

"You know dats right."

"Don't worry as soon as you get me to da school building I'ma fuck you up."

"You promise?" she says with a sexy smile.

"Wit out a doubt."

"I gave Daniels somethin for you. She goin get it to you later. I'ma get you to da school building tomorrow so you can make good on ya promise," Mi-Mi tells me then becomes quiet because Daniels is approaching.

When Daniels walks up I excuse myself and walk back to where Heem is standing. When I look back up to the desk they are both laughing and looking at me, Heem notices it and I can tell that he finally believes me.

Later I'm coming out of the shower and I notice Daniels watching me. I'm in my cell in my boxers putting lotion on when Daniels opens my door and stands there. She looks down and I follow her gaze and realize that my dick is partially out of the slit in my boxers. I let her look for a few seconds before I fix myself. She lifts her eyes and stops at the scar that runs from my waist to my neckline.

"What happened to you?"

"I got shot. Doctors had to open my chest to save me."

Daniels looks around for a minute then reaches inside her shirt between two buttons that were undone and pulls out a brown paper bag and tosses it to me.

"That's from Mi-Mi she said give her a call tonight." Daniels walks off after relaying the message to me. It confuses me a little until I look in the bag.

Inside the bag is another zip-lock bag of weed, five packs of cigarettes and the cell phone I had asked for. Attached to the phone is a note. The note is just a message from Rosie telling me to contact her as soon as I get the phone but at the bottom of the note there was a different handwriting and a reminder from Mi-Mi telling me to call her also. Along with the reminder is an assurance that she would have the charger for me the next time we met at the school building.

I get dressed and take a portion of the weed out and wrap it in toilet paper. I put the weed and one of the packs of cigarettes in my pocket and walk out of the cell. Heem is on the phone when I come out and I wait for him to be done.

When he finishes with his call Heem walks over to me and

I lead him to his cell where I give him the weed and the cigarettes. We sit there talking for about an hour until it's time to lock in and before I go I get some food from him because I know that I'm going to have the munchies later.

When I lock in my cell I get high with my celly and even though the weed gets the job done I wish it was wet which is my drug of choice. I've had some hellified experiences on wet and I wish that that was what I was smoking. I remind myself to tell Rosie to send me some with the next package. I finish getting high, then I pullout the phone to call my oldhead.

Chapter 8

JUNE 1993

It was beautiful the day that I was released from the hospital. Rosie, Tone and Lisette were all there to bring me home and it felt good to be leaving the hospital in one piece. I wasn't 100% yet but I was healthy enough to go home. I had been in the hospital for three weeks awaiting this day.

The doctor warned me that I wasn't to indulge in anything too strenuous and informed me that that included sports, work or sex. He said that it would be at least another two weeks before my body would be back to full strength and warned me to take it easy during that time.

Wanting to make sure that I would be well taken care of Rosie insisted that I stay at her house and I accepted. After what had happened with my mom I didn't want to be around her let alone live under the same roof with her. Rosie told Lisette that she was welcome to stay there also and she said that she would ask her parents. Even though she was 18 and could do whatever she wanted Lisette had a great respect for her parents and the fact that she was still living under their roof.

When we arrived at Rosie's and I got out of the car the first thing I noticed was how busy the corner was. Business was flowing everywhere and the workers were taking care of business efficiently. I had been cooped up in a hospital for three weeks and wasn't ready to go into the house yet so I told Rosie that I was going to sit on the steps.

I could tell that she wanted to protest but she didn't. Instead she went inside and returned with a pillow for me to sit on and told me to come inside if I did not feel good. She went back inside and I sat on the steps and Lisette sat in between my legs while Tone went down the street to check on things. When he was gone I draped my arms over Lisette's shoulders and felt her pregnant stomach. She was four months already and while her stomach wasn't huge she was showing. I rubbed her stomach and she kissed my arm.

"I'm so glad you home papi," she purred.

"I'm glad to be home."

"My mom says you have to come by the house when you're better."

"Tell her I will."

While I listened to her talk I realized how lucky I was to have a girl like Lisette. She had been by my bedside everyday since I was moved from the ICU. She hadn't been going to school but her parents hadn't said anything because they understood the severity of what had happened to me. It didn't really matter anyway because Lisette had gained enough credits to graduate so no one was really concerned with her missing the days.

As I sat there I began to have a nervous feeling inside of me. Something just didn't feel right. It seemed as if everybody that walked past me looked at me crazy like they were going to do something to me and I suddenly didn't feel safe sitting on the steps. My hands trembled slightly and Lisette noticed it and asked me what was wrong. I told her that I was fine then called Tone who was talking to one of the workers. He signaled for me to wait a second and when he was done talking he came to see what I wanted.

"What you need yo?" Tone asked me.

"Give me ya gun."

"For what?"

"Somethin don't feel right."

"Pooh you home now, you safe." Tone tried to assure me.

"Nigga dis where I got shot at. Just give me da gun."

Tone looked at me then at Lisette as if asking for her approval.

"Yo I asked you for da gun not her. What you lookin at her for?"

"Whateva," Tone said and pulled his gun off his waist and handed it to me. I sat it on the steps next to me and watched Tone walk back towards the corner.

I scanned the street again making sure that there was no one lurking or waiting for me. Once I felt that I was safe I turned back to Lisette who had a concerned look on her face. I knew that there was something that she wanted to say but she didn't she just snuggled up to me and told me that she loved me.

Later that night Lisette had gone to her house to talk to her parents and I was still sitting on the steps watching the corner operate. It was dark and Mama walked up and sat next to me. We really didn't know each other at the time aside from Tone introducing us but that night we got well acquainted with one another. We sat and talked and during our third hour of conversation, we were like brother and sister. During the time that we had been talking Lisette had come back with enough clothes for at least a week but when she arrived all I did was give her a peck on the cheek before jumping back into my conversation with Mama.

It wasn't until her little brother walked up that we took an extended break in our talking. Mama said that she had to take care of something but would be right back. When she left I sat by myself thinking about what I could do next.

I knew that I had two options. The first which was leaving the streets alone would seem the correct choice to most people. I mean after all I had come face to face with death and lived to tell about it. There was one problem with this choice however, and that problem was that I was no longer like most people. I was a hoodlum now and I couldn't see myself going back to school, or getting a job and making minimum wage while trying to support my girl and my baby which was on the way. This was not an option in my mind.

Once I realized this I knew that option two was the way that I was going to go. I was going to take my near death experience as a lesson and learn from it. I was going to keep it moving. I was going to be a hustla. I had already had a taste of the life I could lead if I succeeded and there was no way that I was going to settle for less when I had more being handed to me on a silver platter.

In all reality it would have been easy for me to give up the streets after I got shot. It would have been easy for me to go back to school and readjust myself into a normal life but the truth was I didn't want to. I had gotten a taste of money and power and that's like a wild animal that has been domesticated getting its first taste of blood. There's no turning back and that was exactly how I felt sitting on those steps that night.

This wasn't even a decision that I had to struggle with. In fact the choice that I would have to make when Mama returned would be harder than me deciding what direction I should steer my life in.

Mama came back twenty minutes later with a rolled blunt. She lit the blunt and instantly I could tell that it wasn't weed that she was smoking. The smell was different and the blunt was way too small to have weed in it. She took a few pulls on the blunt then began to continually lick her lips. I became intrigued and wanted to know what she was smoking.

"Que eso?" I said in Spanish asking her what it was.

"Tu habla espanol?" She responded asking me did I speak Spanish.

"Un pocito," I said letting her know I only spoke a little.

"Algo mojau," she responded.

"What?" I asked in English and she laughed.

"I thought you spoke Spanish?"

"I told you I only spoke a little."

"Who taught you?"

"Rosie taught me a little bit while I was in da hospital."

"You still wanna learn?"

"I don't care."

"Okay, first lesson. Algo mojau means something wet."

Now I was confused. That was the response she had given me when I asked her what was in the blunt and now that I knew that it meant something wet I still did not know what she was smoking.

"Aiight so what you smoking?"

"Somethin wet."

"What?"

"Somethin wet. Wet," she said adding emphasis on wet but I still didn't know what she was talking about and my facial expression must have relayed my confusion.

"Aye dio mio," she huffed. "Wet, angel dust," she said and I finally understood.

"Don't dat shit make you crazy?" I asked her.

"No stupid ass."

"What it do to you?"

"Here try it," she said and tried to pass me the blunt but I didn't accept and she smiled before pulling it back and taking another pull.

I had heard some crazy stories about niggas and what they had done when they were under the influence of angel dust. Mama continued to smoke the blunt until it was gone and when it was she pulled another blunt and a small cellophane packet out of her pocket. She cracked the blunt then dumped the contents of the cellophane packet into it.

I asked her what it was and she told me that it was the dust. The contents of it were so miniscule that I wondered if it could actually get anybody high. With how much was in the packet it was no wonder that Mama was getting ready to smoke another blunt. I found myself thinking that maybe wet wasn't so bad and then I actually found myself thinking about smoking some. Mama caught me looking at her and laughed.

"Yo what's up wit you bro?"

"What dat shit make you feel like?"

"Just try it."

"I don't know bout dat."

"I got you. I ain't goin let nothin happen to you," she said as she lit the skinny blunt.

She took four deep pulls then handed it to me and

I took it but didn't hit it. Instead I just looked at it. I stared at it for about a minute then the moment of truth came and I took my first puff of angel dust. I was cautious with the first puff. Then I took another and another and before I knew it I had hit the blunt six times before I handed it back.

For the first few minutes I didn't feel anything, then out of the blue I found myself licking my lips continuously like I had seen Mama doing and I understood why she was doing it. The wet made you feel like you couldn't feel your lips. I licked and licked and no matter how many times I did I still couldn't feel my lips. It wasn't like weed. I didn't have cotton mouth. My mouth was still moist. I just couldn't feel my lips. Mama handed me the blunt again and I took it and hit it again until there was nothing left. I smoked a cigarette after it and when I was done I stood to stretch my legs and almost fell flat on my face.

It was like the entire Hancock Street was spinning. Mama noticed me off balance and grabbed my arm to steady me. She was laughing the whole time and now that the wet had taken full effect on me I found nothing funny. My eyes were open but I couldn't see anything but lights and silhouettes. Mama kept her hand on my arm and tried to get me to sit down but I didn't want to so she asked me to walk to the corner with her so she could get a soda from Santos' store. I agreed and when I took my first step it felt like I was weightless. I grabbed onto Mama who was still laughing and used her for support. She led me down the street to the store laughing the entire way.

When we got to the store I heard Tone's voice but couldn't see him because the wet had me blinded. Tone was chastising one of the workers for something he had done and when he finished he cursed to himself in Spanish.

"What's wrong with him?" he asked after noticing me and Mama. I could hear the alarm in his voice and I assumed that the alarm was because I had just got out of the hospital.

"Nothin wrong wit him," Mama responded. "Tone, I can't see," I said.

"What do you mean you can't see?"

"I can't see."

"Que le esiste Mama?" he said asking her what she had done to me.

"I didn't do nothin to him."

"Why he actin crazy den?"

"He wetted," she told him.

"What?"

"He smoked some wet with me."

Tone was silent for a minute and I assume he was looking at my condition then he burst out laughing. Everybody was finding this funny except me. The wet had me feeling crazy and at that moment I prayed to God to let me sober up. I promised him that I would never get high again if he would just let my high come down. Not only did God not answer my prayer but it was like he punished me because my high seemed to boost.

Mama told Tone to watch me while she went into the store and I felt her release my arm. I wobbled and stumbled and before I knew it I was on my ass on the filthy concrete. Tone laughed even harder and I struggled to get to my feet. When I realized that I wasn't going to be able to get to my feet on my own I asked for Tone's help but for some reason he acted like he didn't know what I was talking about.

I asked him three times and after every time he asked me what the fuck I was talking about. It wouldn't be until the following day that I would learn that while I was on the ground no one could understand me because all I did was mutter unintelligible words and phrases. In my head I was telling Tone to help me up off of the ground but to his ears it sounded like this: @&#^% #^$%& #^#@.

Eventually Tone and Mama stopped laughing long enough to help me up off the ground and get me to Rosie's house where she too laughed at my condition. I was high as shit that night. I don't remember anything past Rosie laughing at me. I don't remember how I got up the steps or to the room that Rosie had set up for us or even how I got in the bed. All I remember was telling myself that I never wanted to get wetted again and promising myself that I wouldn't. That would be a promise that I would break exceptionally fast.

APHILLYATION & 5 STAR SCRIBES PUBLISHING PRESENTS

* * * * *

Two days after being released from the hospital I was back on the strip. I argued with Rosie, Lisette and Mama who had appointed herself my guardian angel but in the end I won. They all tried to discourage me from returning so quickly but I wasn't trying to hear none of what they were talking. They finally gave up knowing that I was going to do what I wanted regardless of what they said. The only one who didn't try to stop me was Tone and that was because he was a hustla just like me.

Tone knew I would be alright back on the strip. It wasn't like I was the one doing the hustling. I was the caseworker. I made sure the workers had the drugs. I collected the money. I was the one who made sure that all of the numbers were correct and that everything came in straight. I didn't have the hassle of dealing with the fiends or nothing like that so I knew that I'd be fine.

Mama, who since she couldn't convince me to stay in the house, decided to stay on the strip with me while I handled my shift. I really ain't mind though because she was funny and cool to be around not to mention that she had promised to keep helping me with my Spanish lessons.

The afternoon was flying and the money was coming in at a rapid pace. Having Mama out there with me actually paid off because the strip was moving so fast that there were a few times when I almost couldn't keep up. It wasn't because I didn't know what I was doing, I was a seasoned vet at this time. It was because being shot and not fully recovering was taking a toll on me. Mama helped me keep up and when my shift was done I was dead tired. I dragged myself to Rosie's where I flopped down the sofa as soon as I was close enough to it.

I had just drifted off to sleep when I heard the phone ringing in the distance. It eventually stopped ringing and a few minutes after it did Rosie came running into the living room. She woke me up and told me that I was about to be a uncle. I looked up at her like she was crazy not understanding what she was talking about. It took a few seconds to shake off the sleep that I had just been drifting into and when I did I finally understood that she was telling me that Rebecca was about to have her baby.

I sat up and Rosie said something about coming right back. When she did she had Lisette with her and they were telling me to get up so we could go to the hospital to be with her. I reluctantly got up and followed them out of the house to witness what Lisette would be going through in a few months.

Chapter 9

FEBRUARY 2001

C.F.C.F UNIT D2-1

I listen while Daniels calls out the names of the people who received mail over the intercom. I was one of the last names called. I walk to the desk and was handed eight pieces of mail. Six of the eight pieces were cards. My birthday was yesterday. As I look at the return addresses I am almost shocked to see that both Spud and Tone have sent me cards, especially since we haven't been speaking to each other, or at least that's what I thought.

As I read the cards they sent me it is obvious that they both have been communicating with one another. Both cards wish me a happy 23rd birthday and they both end with Spud and Tone saying that they love me and this makes me smile. Regardless of what we are or were going through I still love both of them like they are my brothers which they are. These are the only two niggas that I trust with my life and there is no doubt in my mind that the feeling is mutual.

I look at the cards some more and realize that it is time for me to stop being stubborn and reconnect with my brothers. I go straight to my cell and get a pen and paper and think about what I am going to say. While the purpose of this letter is to reconnect there are still things regarding our case that need to be said and I feel as

though I have to say them and I intend to say them. I take a deep breath and begin writing Spud.

> Spud,
>
> What's up homie? I got your card today wishing me a happy birthday and I appreciated the gesture. It's been a while since the last time we spoke and I'll take partial blame for that because I know that you felt as though I was trying to lay all of the blame at your feet with the comments that I made but that wasn't the case. I was laying a big portion of the blame at your feet and I did that because at that time I felt that if it hadn't been for your greed that we wouldn't have been in that position and to tell you the truth I still feel the same way now that I did the last time we spoke.

With that said, understand that you my brother and regardless of what I say or think I love you. Brothers are allowed to disagree and have different opinions but at the end of the day ain't nothing supposed to be able to come between us and we allowed this situation that we in to come between us. This is the first communication that we had in eleven months and that is unacceptable.

Like I said I still feel that you should own a nice chunk of the blame but I'm not willing to let you not doing so come in between us. You been my man since we was 8 years old and I would kill for you and just as quickly lay my life on the line for you and I know that you would do the same for me. Let's put the nut shit behind us and focus on this case that we got in front of us and act like the family we is.

I'ma write Tone and tell him the same thing so I can be back at peace with my brothers. Write me back when you get this.

POOH

LOVE IS ALWAYS GOIN BE LOVE

I write Tone the same letter that I wrote Spud then I put them into their respective envelopes and sit them on the table.

I would mail them later. I glance out my door and seeing that the coast is clear I light a cigarette and think about my brothers. I love them both and would do anything for them. The main reason that we haven't been speaking is because I was extra vocal with why I thought we ended up killing that cop.

I'm glad that I wrote the letters because I want them to understand that no matter what I say I still got major genuine love for them. I finish my cigarette and decide to call Rebecca. I put the towel up to cover my door and pull out my cell phone. As always she answers on the second ring.

"Hello . . ."

"Becca what's up . . ."

"Oh my god Pooh what's up baby . . ."

"Chillin, how you doin . . ."

"I'm good why you ain't been callin me . . ."

"I been busy . . ."

"In jail. Come on Pooh you can do betta den dat .."

"You know me and Spud wasn't seein eye to eye."

"What dat got to do wit me? We family just cause you and him ain't getting along don't mean you ain't pose to talk to me . . ."

"I know my bad. I called cause of Spud. I just wrote him a letter but I want you to do me a favor. . .

"Anything. What you need . . ."

"Did he call you today yet . . ."

"Nope he always call at night . . ."

"Aiight when he call I want you to call me on three way . . ."

"Call you how . . ."

"I got a cell phone . . ."

"In jail . . ."

"Yeah. Here take da number 267-434-2478. You got dat. . ."

"Yeah I got it . . ."

"Good make sure dat as soon as he call you call me . . ."

"I will. I'll dial your number before I accept the call . . ."

"Cool. I gotta go Becca I gotta charge da phone . .

"Okay I'll make sure we call tonight . . ." "Aiight . . ."

"Pooh . . ."

"What's up . . ."

"I love you . . ."

"I love you too lil sis . . ." I say and end the call.

Soon as I hang up the phone someone knocks on my door and I go to the door to see who it is. I keep the phone in my hand in case it's a set-up so I can flush it down the toilet. I slide the towel to the side a little and look out the door and it's Heem.

"Open da door nigga."

I press the call button and Daniels buzzes the door and it opens. Heem comes in my cell sweating and breathing heavily and I immediately think he was fighting. He catches his breath then drinks some water out of my sink.

"You aiight nigga?" I ask.

"Yeah I'm good. Yo come play ball wit me."

"What?"

"Its two niggas in da yard dat wanna play for some money."

"So play wit one of dem niggas you play wit every day."

"Not for no bread."

"Come on man you know I don't like associatin wit deez

niggas."

"You ain't gotta associate you just gotta help me bust dey ass."

"Come on dog I ain't played no ball in almost two years. I'm all outta shape."

"So what you got game dat shit like ridin a bike."

Knowing that Heem ain't going to let up I finally relent. I shake my head and sit down and pull my boots off and reach for my sneakers. Heem smiles then says that he'll meet me in the yard. I tie my sneakers, tuck my phone then head out of my cell.

When I get to the yard Heem is talking shit while the two niggas that we're suppose to play are shooting around. Heem notices me and calls for the ball to be checked.

"Game sixteen straight," he says and our opponents agree. The ball is checked and the game is on.

I used to have a nice game. Well let me clear that up. I had a nice jump shot at one point and an And One handle before And One existed but now I don't know. Heem passes me the ball and I take a wide open shot that ends up being an air ball and I look at Heem like. 'I told you so.'

Our opponents get the ball and run six straight points off on us before Heem steals a pass and scores for us. I get the ball again and shoot and I get a lucky shooter roll then I decide to play a different game. Noticing that I need time for my shot to start hitting I decide to use my dribble which has no rust on it at all.

It takes me about ten seconds to realize that the nigga sticking me can't stay in front of me and from there it's on. Our opponents get the ball again twice but they don't score and the score ends up being sixteen to six. Being the gambler that he is Heem allows them to run it back twice. The second game is a little more competitive because I am tired as is Heem and the score is sixteen to twelve us but the third game is a blowout. After the second game everyone is tired so we take a few minutes to get a breather and that is definitely a bad move on their behalf. The third game my jump shot is on and I hit seven in a row to start the game which we end up winning sixteen to four. Heem tells one of them to only give him half of what he is owed and we head back onto the block. I am dead tired and all I want to do is take a shower and relax. On my way to my cell Daniels spots me and calls me to the desk.

"What's up?" I ask as I approach.

"Mi-Mi said don't come to the church tonight she gotta leave early. She said call her later." "Aught." I say and turn to walk off.

"I ain't know you play ball."

"A lil," I say and keep walking.

When I get to my cell I strip out of my sweaty clothes and get my shower stuff together. Before leaving I check my phone and notice that my chick from Virginia called. I make a note to myself to call her back and head to the shower.

* * * * *

It's close to 9:00 P.M. when Heem comes to my cell with a bowl of tuna fish. He sits the bowl on the table then sits on the toilet and lights a cigarette. He smokes half then passes it to me and I hand him the phone. Every night around this time Heem comes to my cell to use the phone and call whoever it was that he calls. I put the cigarette out and grabbed the bowl of tuna just as he was greeting the person he was calling.

I put my headphones on so I won't hear his conversation and begin to make tuna sandwiches. I'm on my third sandwich when Heem gets my attention by waving his hand at me. I take the headphones off and he tells me that another call is incoming. He tells whoever he is talking to to hold on and I check the caller ID seeing that it is Rebecca which means that Spud is on the line with her. I tell Heem that I gotta take the call and he tells his party that he'll call them back. I tell him to give me a few minutes then come back and he exits the cell. I take a deep breath then answer the call. "Yo . . ." I say answering the phone.

"Pooh . . ." Spud said.

"Yeah it's me . . ."

"What's up . . ."

"You tell me . . ."

"I'm chillin . . ."

"Dats what's up, I wrote you a letter today . . ." "Yeah you get my card . . ."

"Yeah I got it good lookin . . ."

"So what's up nigga why it took so long for you to get wit me . . ."

"You know why . . ."

"Dats why you ain't holla at me cause we had an argument . . ." Spud asked as if he can't believe that that was the reason for us not speaking. "Yeah . . ." I respond.

"Yo dog, fuck dat shit. You my family. I don't care what we argue bout. We ain't pose to let dat make us stop talkin. We bout to fight da biggest case in da city and we ain't speakin like some girls. I love you nigga and yeah I was mad when you said dat it was my fault but it was a lot my fault. I just ain't wanna hear it at da time . . ."

"I feel you homie. You know I'm stubborn but you right. We trippin over some nut shit. What's up wit Tone . . ."

"He cool. I got a letter from him da other day. . ." "I got a card from him too . . ."

"Of course you did nigga we ya brothers . . ."

"Ain't no doubt. So what's up wit da case . . ."

"We goin to jail dog. I just ain't sure if we goin get life or da death penalty yet . . ."

"Yo I wrote you a letter but I gotta change it cause I got a plan but I don't wanna say it over da phone so when you get my letter holla right back and let me know what you think . . ."

"Aiight. You been talkin to Rosie . . ."

"Yeah, I talk to her every couple days. Why what's up . ."

"Nothin, I just wanted to make sure you was in contact wit her . . ."

"You don't be talkin to her . . ."

"Only when I need somethin . . ."

"What y'all beefin . . ."

"Na I'm just on my jail house shit. You know I don't really be talkin to nobody when I'm biddin . . ." I knew exactly what he was talking about. When he did his first bid he only called home when he needed something. Other than that he wrote periodically but that was it.

"You cool you need somethin . . ." I ask him.

"Na nigga I'm good. You ain't da only one dat stacked some paper . . ."

The recording on his end informed us that we only had a minute left to talk so we began to say our goodbyes.

"Yo I love you dog. I'ma get wit you later dis week . . ." Spud says.

"Yo call me at dis number around dis time wheneva you want and tell Tone da same thing . . ."

"Aiight I got you . . ."

"I love you dog . . ."

"I love you too . . ." Spud responds then the phone cuts off.

I shut my cell phone off and slowly a smile appears on my face. I know that it's my fault that I hadn't been speaking to Spud or Tone but I am so stubborn that sometimes it clouds my judgement. I'm thinking clearly now and I am glad that I am because I have finally reconciled with one of my brothers and I am sure that I will do the same with the other very soon. I have only one other thing left to do and that is to get us all in the same jail and I think I know just how to do that. There is nothing I can do today so I decide to relax. Then I realize that I am supposed to call my Virginia chick back.

Ronnie short for Veronica is four years my senior and she

is like a landmark in my life. I say this because Ronnie is the first female that I ever cheated on Lisette with. That was seven years ago and even though we have never had a stable relationship with each other she still loves me and in my own little special way I love her too. I'm just not in love with her. I can still remember the day I met her like it was yesterday.

* * * * *

SEPTEMBER 1993

The Puerto Rican Day Parade, one of the biggest days in our neighborhood and it was jumping. Me and Tone were at 5th and Lehigh gassing up Rosie's Lexus which we were driving for the day and while Tone pumped the gas I watched the traffic flow by. There were cars everywhere with niggas and bitches hanging out of the windows. Ours was not as big as New York's parade but it was still a beautiful thing.

Just as Tone was finished pumping the gas a Jeep Cherokee with four girls in it pulled up to the pump next to ours. I watched as the driver got out to stretch her legs. The sight of her captivated me. She was about an inch taller than me and her honey brown legs were full and beautiful under the white tennis skirt that she wore. Her titties strained against the yellow and white Polo shirt that she wore which matched her yellow and white Nikes and her shoulder length hair with bangs accentuating her pretty face was tied into a ponytail with a yellow scrunchie.

I watched her go into the gas station then come back out and begin pumping the gas. She looked over at me and smiled and I returned the gesture. Our eyes locked for a second and this was the first time since I had gotten with Lisette that I found myself attracted to another female. She shied away from our stare down before I did but did so with a gorgeous smile.

"Go talk to her nigga," Tone said startling me and dragging me out of the trance that she had me in.

"What you talkin bout?" I asked him.

"Come on nigga. Y'all starin at each other like some romance movie or some shit."

"Whateva nigga let's go," I said and opened the door to get into the car.

"What you scared?"

"Scared of what?"

"Of her."

"Nigga she ain't even worryin bout me," I tell Tone and as soon as I do she calls out to me.

"What you goin do now?" Tone asked as he leaned against the car smiling.

I looked at Tone then at the female and walked over to her car. She took the nozzle out of her car and put it back on the pump then looked at me with a beautiful set of light brown eyes.

"What's up?" I asked her.

"What's up with you?"

"I'm chillin. What you call me for?"

"Why you say it like that?"

"Cause I was gettin ready to leave when you stopped me."

"I ain't mean to bother you. I just wanted to know if maybe you wanted to hang out."

"Wit you?"

"Yeah, wit me."

"What about ya friends?"

"Dey can come and ya friend can come too." "Where you wanna hang out at?"

"I don't know. I'm not from here."

"Where you from?"

"Virginia."

"What you doin all da way up here?"

"My girlfriend brought us up here for the parade."

As if on cue a Puerto Rican girl stuck her head out of the rear window of the jeep and asked her friend what was taking her so long. Seeing me she simply said, 'Oh.' She was getting ready to pull her head back in when the chick that I was talking to stopped her.

"Marie where's a good place for us to hang out?" "Who?"

"Us, all of us," she said making it a point to point at me.

"We could go down Penns Landing."

"Penns Landing," she said to me as if she was asking my approval and I shrugged my shoulders letting her know that it didn't matter to me.

"Alright Penns Landing it is. We'll follow you." "Cool wit me," I said and walked back to Rosie's car.

"What's goin on?" Tone asked as I got in the car.

"We goin to Penns Landing," I told him. "Who?"

"All of us," I told him and he smiled.

"I guess you wasn't scared."

* * * * *

We walked, talked and smoked weed until me and Tone's

legs were too tired to walk any further and the females were too high. When we decided to sit, me and the chick who had talked to me in the first place sat at a bench a couple of benches away from Tone and the other three females. The entire time we had been walking, the conversation had been on more of a comedic level but I knew that it was now going to turn more personal and I was ready for that.

While me and Tone were in the car together he told me exactly how to handle conversation and the advice that he gave me was to lie and that's what I did. When she asked me how old I was I told her that I was 18 even though I didn't look it. She seemed to buy it and actually made a comment about me having a baby face. When she asked me if I went to college I told her no which wasn't a lie but then I told her that I worked for my uncle's car lot which was a lie. That's how it went for the hour that we sat on the bench. She asked a question and I told her a lie. Then I would ask her a question and after knowing her for a while I would learn that she was answering my questions honestly.

I learned that her name was Veronica or Ronnie which was what she liked to be called. She was nineteen, from Virginia and a second year student at Georgetown University. She was majoring in journalism with the hopes of writing for a magazine such as Time or another periodical of that magnitude. She told me that the three girls with her all went to college with her and that the one who had suggested Penns Landing was actually from Philly. It was her that had convinced them to come to the city for the parade. After many questions from each of us a brief silence ensued.

Neither of us said anything for a few seconds. Instead we just looked at each other then she leaned in to kiss me. Instinctively I tried to pull away but she grabbed the back of my neck and pressed her mouth against mine sliding her tongue into my mouth. Her kiss was tender. I felt myself succumbing to it and before I knew it we were swapping spit like it was going out of style. One of her friends called her and Ronnie pulled back to respond.

Her friend, a dark-skinned black girl waved Ronnie over and she got up off of the bench and walked to her. They conversed for a few minutes then Ronnie came back to the bench and asked me what we were going to do next. I told her that I didn't care and she suggested that me, her, the dark skinned chick and Tone go somewhere where we could all chill alone. I looked over at her friend who was still standing in the same place only now Tone was beside her and they were feeling all over one another.

I understood what was being suggested but I wasn't sure if I wanted to indulge. Tone stopped feeling on the dark-skinned chick long enough to ask me what we were going to do. He had a look on his face that told me that he wanted me to go along with the plan so I relented even though I wasn't sure if I really wanted to. Ronnie told her friend and Tone that it was on. Then the two females went to tell their other friends what was going on.

When they walked away Tone walked over to me and smiled.

"What's up wit you. Why you lookin sad?" Tone asked me.

"I don't know bout dis."

"What?"

"Deez chicks. I got a girl."

"Dats why you trippin?"

"Yeah."

"Dat shit don't mean nothin. Everybody get pussy on da side."

"But I love Lisette."

"And all da niggas dat get pussy on da side love dey bitches too. It's just part of da game."

"What you talkin bout?"

"Pooh you gettin money. Now all types of bitches goin be on ya dick. Dey already on ya dick but you don't be payin attention."

"You trippin."

"No you trippin. I be watchin da lil bitches on da block and some of da older bitches and dey all wanna fuck you."

"So what. I got a girl."

"Man fuck all dat. Deez bitches wanna fuck tonight and dats what we goin do. Dem bitches from Virginia we ain't neva gain see dem again anyway."

"I guess you right."

"You know I'm right." Tone said and nudged me then nodded towards the chicks who were coming back.

"We riding with you guys?" Ronnie asked and

Tone nodded his head yes then we all headed to Rosie's Lexus.

* * * * *

When I awoke the next morning I was ass naked as was Ronnie who was laying on her stomach with half of the sheet covering her. In the bed next to ours Tone and the dark skinned chick were in the same position as us except the darkskinned chick had no sheet over her and I could see every inch of her ebony colored nakedness. I yawned then sat up, grabbed my boxers and slid them on. I got a cigarette out of my pack and lit it smoking while looking at Ronnie who looked truly amazing naked. It was like she sensed me looking at her because she awoke and our eyes met and she smiled at me.

"What's up?" she asked me.

"Chillin. What's up wit you?"

"Chillin. I had a good time last night."

"Me too," I told her.

"When we goin do it again?"

"I don't know bout dat."

She sat up and covered herself with the sheet. "Pooh, I know you probably got a girl or something and that's cool. I'm not trying to come between that. I like you though and I just want to be able to get together from time to time. I can come to Philly or you can come to Virginia whichever makes you more comfortable. I just want to be able to see you on occasion."

Right then and there I had acquired my first side chick and she would outlast any other side chick that I would ever have. We lay there talking for about twenty minutes before Tone and his chick woke up. Everyone got up and got dressed then left the motel. We drove them to the Northeast to their friends house and before she got out of the car me and Ronnie exchanged numbers as did Tone and the dark skinned chick. We both gave them Rosie's number.

When we got to the block it was eleven o'clock in the morning and Mama was on the corner making sure that everything ran smooth. She seen us and shook her head.

"Where y'all been?"

"Out." Tone responded.

"Since yesterday?"

"Yeah. "

"Whores," she stated, then walked off.

Me and Tone headed to Rosies but after hearing Mama's statement I couldn't help but think that she knew what me and Tone were up to. Knowing how close her and Lisette had become over the past few months I couldn't help but wonder if she would tell her of what she suspected. I decided that after I took a shower and changed my clothes I would go talk to her and find out.

* * * * *

"Mama let me talk to you," I said as I walked up to the steps she was sitting on with about five other females. She told me to wait a minute and I told her that I would be right back. I walked to my car to get my cigarettes then headed back to the steps. I hadn't been able to talk to her earlier because I had fallen asleep, then had to wake up and work my shift. I looked around for her all day but she was nowhere to be found until now.

My beeper said that it was 1:12 in the morning but that meant nothing in my hood. There was always something going on.

On my way back to the steps I saw Mama coming towards me. When she reached me she hugged me and took the cigarette I was smoking. She puffed it twice then handed it back and pulled a blunt from behind her ear.

"What you wanna talk about?" she asked.

"I wanna know if you goin keep what you and Tone talked about earlier between us."

"What you talkin bout?" she asked.

"Remember when you called us whores."

Mama started laughing and I wondered what was so funny. She laughed for a few seconds then lit her blunt which she puffed twice then handed to me. I accepted the wet blunt then she laughed again.

"What's so funny?" I asked her.

"You."

"Me?"

"Yeah you. You all scared and shit dat Lisette goin find out dat you was gettin some pussy on da side."

"Ain't nobody scared."

"Yes you is. Dats why you tryin to see if I'ma say somethin."

"Is you?"

"I thought you wasn't scared."

"Is you goin say somethin or not?"

"No I ain't goin say nothin stupid ass. Dats your business not mine and besides I knew it was gonna happen sooner or later."

"How you know dat?"

"Please, all deez bitches on ya dick."

"What bitches you talkin bout?" I asked. "Damn near all da bitches in da neighborhood. Deez bitches be waitin for you to try to fuck em but you always be up under Lisette ass."

"You trippin."

"No you trippin. Dem bitches I was just sitting wit all wanna give you some pussy but dey leave you alone cause I make em."

"Why you make em?"

"Cause I know you all in love but I knew dat sooner or later you was goin stray and now dat you did I'ma let my girls know so dey can get what dey want."

"Yo, don't do dat. Dis was a one time thing."

"If you say so. Gimmie my blunt," she said and I handed it back to her.

"T-i."

"It is."

"No it ain't Pooh. You a guy and guy's is assholes. You goin cheat again and again and again. It ain't nothin wrong wit it. Just don't neva put none of dem bitches before Lisette."

"Whateva," I said and turned walking away.

"Whateva my ass," Mama said and headed back to the steps where her friends were.

Chapter 10

FEBRUARY 2001

C.F.C.F UNIT D2-1

"Nevins visit" I open my door and hold my finger up letting Daniels know that I'll be there in a minute. I finish brushing my freshly cut hair then exit the cell closing the door behind me. Ronnie is here to see me today and it is the first time that I will have seen her in about a year. After talking to her the other day she insisted on coming to see me and I told her to come. She had been wanting to come for the past few months but I wouldn't let her because I only get an hour a week and the hour is always taken up by Lisette and my kids.

Just recently I found out that if someone came to see you from out of state that you would be granted an extra hour. When I learned of this I immediately told Ronnie to come. The last time I had seen her was about two months before I caught my case. She had come to Philly for the weekend and we hung out for the two days that she was here promising to get together again soon. I would have never guessed that we wouldn't be able to keep that promise.

I get my pass from Daniels then head to the visiting room. It's not as crowded as it usually is and within two minutes of arriving I am sitting in one of the metal seats waiting for my visit to be escorted in. A few dudes that I recognize are on the dance floor and they either say what's up or give me a head nod and I subtly return the gestures. A minute or two into my wait the door opens and in comes a bunch of visitors, among them is Ronnie. I look at her and simply smile. She has grown even more beautiful over the years and it amazes me that we managed to keep our relationship going this long.

"Hey boo," she says as she approaches after giving the guard at the desk her visitors pass.

"What's up," I say opening my arms accepting her into a warm embrace.

We share a passionate kiss then release each other. I look her up and down admiring her figure which has only enhanced since we first met and she spins around giving me a great view of her great body. Finally we sit down next to one another. She immediately takes my hand into hers.

"How you been? I missed you so much."

"I been aiight. Tryin to figure out what's goin happen wit dis case."

"How's it looking?"

"You want da truth or a lie?"

"When we start lying to each other?"

"It don't look too good."

"What your lawyer say?"

"Ain't really too much he can say da case is so crazy dat he sayin it'll be a miracle if we get life."

"Are you serious? There has to be something he can do. You know my girlfriend is in law school. Maybe I could have her look at your case."

I smiled seeing the worry on her face but I knew that what she was offering was worthless.

"Ronnie I got one of the best lawyers on da East

Coast so believe me when I say there's nothing dat can be done."

"Pooh don't say that. You can never stop fighting."

"I ain't said nothin bout not fightin. I'm just realistic enough to know dat I'm fightin a losing battle."

"What makes you say that?"

"I can't really get into it but trust me shit ain't in my favor. Fuck all dat though cause I know you ain't drive all da way up here to talk bout no depressing shit."

"What's going to happen to you ain't depressing to me. Pooh I care about you and I care about what happens to you."

"I know and I appreciate it."

"You alright in here. You need anything?"

"Na I'm good."

"I know you are I was just checking though," she says then smiles the smile that captured me the first day we met.

For the rest of the visit we sit and talk about the good times that we had over the past seven years. Towards the end of the visit as we were coming from taking pictures I look up and notice Mi-Mi watching me and Ronnie walking back to our seats. Mi-Mi and I lock eyes and she has a weird look on her face. I smile and she doesn't return the gesture but does start walking in our direction. She approaches just as me and Ronnie sit down.

"What's up Pooh?" Mi-Mi asks.

"Chillin what's up wit you?"

"Nothin. Who's dis?" she asks in reference to Ronnie.

"Dis is Ronnie?"

"She ya girl?"

"Somethin like dat?"

"What dat mean?"

"Exactly what I said."

"Um excuse me," Ronnie said interrupting us. "I don't mean to be rude but our visit is almost over and I drove all the way up here from Virginia to see him so if you don't mind I would like to spend our last few minutes alone."

Mi-Mi looks at Ronnie like she couldn't believe that she has just talked to her like that. Mi-Mi glares at Ronnie for a minute then rolls her eyes at me.

"Whateva," she says and walks off.

"I thought I was your only groupie," Ronnie says with her trademark smile on her face.

"You stupid."

"Pooh you know I love you right?"

"Yeah why?"

"I was thinking and if you get a lot of time I want to move up here so I can be close to you." This shocked me. Ronnie had a good job in Virginia as an editor for a newspaper and I couldn't fathom why she would want to throw that away to move up here just so she could visit me in jail. "You ain't gotta do dat yo."

"I know I don't have to but I want to."

The guard comes over to us and gives Ronnie her slip signaling the end of our visit. We stand and Ronnie wraps her arms around me hugging me tightly. When she pulls back to kiss me I notice that she has tears in her eyes. We kiss and when we're done I wipe her tears and tell her that I'm going to be alright. She nods her head and bites down on her bottom lip.

"Promise me you'll think about what I said about me moving up here."

"I will."

"Promise me."

"I promise."

"Okay, I'll be here every week to see you."

"I'll be waiting."

We hug and kiss again. Then she heads to the open door and before I know it she's gone. I go to the front of the visiting room and within minutes I have been strip searched and I'm on my way back to my block. Mi-Mi is waiting on me in the corridor. As I approach her she falls into step with me. "Who was dat?" she asks.

"I already told you who she was."

"What kind of games is you playin Pooh?"

"What is you talkin bout?"

"I thought we had an agreement about otha bitches."

"Man, I agreed not to have no otha c/o bitch in my face out of respect for you but as far as my chicks from da streets you ain't got no say so in dat."

"Dig dis Pooh I ain't say nothin bout ya babymom cause she gotta come see you but you can't be playin me like no nut."

"Back da fuck up for a minute sweetheart," I tell her as we approach the elevator on d-side. "You got our situation fucked up. We do what we do but I'm a grown ass man and da chicks dat come see me got years in wit me and don't know otha woman come before dem. Between dem it's even a pecking order dat dey under-stand and respect. Don't no woman dictate who I deal wit or how I deal wit em and you betta realize dat real quick." "So what you sayin?"

"I just said it."

"You niggas don't appreciate nothin."

"You goin try to use dat against me."

"It's da truth."

"So what. You gave me a little pussy and brought me some shit in dat shit don't mean nothin."

"It don't."

"Fuck no. It would have happened eventually anyway."

"How?"

"Shorty, I got enough money to get whateva I want from any of deez c/o's."

"Pooh listen . . ." she began but the elevator arrived and I cut her off.

"Yo I gotta go." I said boarding the elevator. "You just goin leave like dat?"

"Yeah cause we drawin right now. I'll get wit you later," I tell her as the doors close. Like I previously said I'm shocked that me and Ronnie are still together. Our second meeting had enough firepower to wreck any kind of relationship we thought we might be able to forge but somehow we managed to survive all that transpired on that fateful day in October.

This day is a day that I'll never forget because not only is it the day that Ronnie found out that everything that I told her during our first meeting was a lie. It was also the day that I almost lost everything that mattered most to me in the entire world.

* * * * *

OCTOBER 1993

"Pooh don't forget you gotta get the car seat from my sisters house," Lisette reminded me as I was preparing to leave her house.

She was still two months away from her delivery date but she was going crazy trying to make sure that everything was in order. This day I had agreed to get a car seat from her sister who had an extra brand new one. This was not something that I really wanted to do because her sister lived in the boondocks but I had promised, so I was stuck.

"Pooh remember dat she leave for work at six so you gotta get there before den."

"I know yo I'll be there" I said then bent to kiss her before I left.

As I left the house it was 1:00 p.m. which meant that I had a few hours before I had to go get the car seat so I planned on going to the block to see what was going on. It took me about ten minutes to get there and when I arrived it was busy as usual. The fiends were swarming, the workers were serving them as fast as they could and amidst all of it Mama was sitting on a milk crate smoking a wet blunt watching everything and everybody.

I parked my car on Cambria Street and as soon as I got out the greetings began. Niggas and bitches alike acknowledged me. I now had eight months in on the block and slowly but surely I had made a place for myself among the young elite of the neighborhood. I mean I was nowhere the level of any of the bosses but amongst the niggas from the ages of 14 to 17 I was at the top of a lot of peoples list. The thing that put me over the top was not the fact that I was in charge of the biggest corner in the hood although that did help. What really boosted me was the rumor that was still flying about me killing the nigga that stomped my mom.

At that time not too many young niggas in the hood had that attached to their name. As a matter of fact not too many of them had any kind of riding attached to their name save for a few fights or something like that. I was becoming respected by a lot of people and it showed more and more everyday.

"Pooh what's up baby?" said a female voice from behind me as I felt a set of arms encircle my waist.

As soon as I felt the arms my heart began to beat faster and I got nervous. I immediately freed myself from the persons grip and spun reaching for my gun. I had my hands on the handle of my gun when I looked up and noticed that it was Meeka who had grabbed me.

"Pooh it's only me," she said with a worried look on her

face.

"Yo don't be fuckin walkin up behind me grabbin me like dat. What da fuck is wrong wit you?"

"My fault. I ain't know you was goin get mad."

"Whateva man. Just don't do dat shit again."

"I won't, I promise. Why you ain't call me last night?"

"Cause I ain't say I would."

"Dats how you goin do me huh? You just goin get me to suck ya dick den push me to da side?"

"I ain't ask you to suck my dick. You offered."

"Dats cause I like you."

"If you like me den stop trippin," I told her. She was about to respond but Mama called out to me before she could.

"Mira Pooh deja a esa puta quieta," Mama shouted to me from across the street.

I laughed but Meeka didn't find anything funny. Even though she was black Meeka knew how to speak Spanish from living in Da Bad Landz all of her life. She put her hands on her hips and sneered at Mama. It was obvious to see that she knew that she had just been called a whore. It wasn't as if it was a lie or anything it was the gods honest truth. Since I had been hustling down here I had heard all kinds of stories about Meeka and they all started and ended with a dick in one of the various holes in her body.

"Yo I gotta go," I said and turned to walk off.

"Dats how you goin do me Pooh?"

"I'll get wit you later," I told her as I headed to where Mama was.

I was beginning to regret fucking with Meeka. Truthfully I only got caught up with her because she offered to suck my dick during the first conversation that we had ever had. After hearing the different stories about how well she sucked dick and her offering the service I couldn't say no.

I ain't goin lie. After Tone and Mama told me about all the bitches that wanted me I took a few days and paid attention to the way the chicks treated me and acted around me and it was clearly obvious that Tone and Mama were right. Chicks did want me and the moment I noticed it I was like a changed man. I began being more cordial to the chicks that hung around the block and as soon as I did they all began offering me all kinds of sexual favors. That was almost a month and a half ago and even though I could have had all of them by now I had only had Meeka and that had only occurred within the last week. Meeka was now getting on my nerves and I knew that I had to get rid of her even though it had only been a week.

"Why you wastin ya time wit dat bitch?" Mama asked as I walked up to her.

"What you talkin bout?"

"You know what I'm talkin bout. I saw her try to hug you when you got out ya car."

"She was just sayin what's up."

"Dat ain't how she usually say what's up?" Mama said and the two females with her laughed. "What you mean?"

"Don't act stupid. I know she been suckin ya little dick."

"She ain't been suckin my dick."

"You gonna lie to me now Pooh?"

I looked at Mama and knew that she knew what was going on so instead of lying to her again I stayed silent and my silence was confirmation enough for her.

"Just like I thought."

"Why you frontin on her for?" I asked Mama. "I ain't frontin on her. It ain't my fault dat she sixteen and sucked all da dicks."

"She ain't suck all da dicks," I said.

"She been suckin dick since she was twelve. Trust me she

sucked all da dicks."

"Anyway," I said changing the conversation. "Where Tone at?"

"I don't know. Probably at Rosie's."

"Aiight I be back."

I walked past Mama and the two females that were with her and as I passed them I notice one of them looking me up and down. I hear her ask Mama about me in Spanish. Then I hear Mama tell her to watch what she says because I speak Spanish. When I look back at the female she is blushing but she is also beautiful. She gives me a smile that lets me know that she is definitely willing if I am. I return her smile then keep going to Rosie's.

Just as I get to Rosie's house she is pulling up and calls out to me.

"Pooh ven ayuda me con esta bolsas," she said and I looked at her because I couldn't understand what she was saying.

This was what had been going on for the past month or so. Rosie, Tone and Mama had all been talking to me in Spanish and I have to admit that it helped me pick up the language faster but there were still certain instances when I didn't understand what they were saying, like now.

"What you say?" I asked her.

"Ven ayuda me con esta bolsas."

"What?" I asked again.

"Aye dio mio come help me with the bags."

"Oh no problem," I said and walked over to the car.

"You still got some learning to do."

"I'm gettin there."

As I was helping Rosie with the grocery bags Tone came to the door with no shirt on and looked up and down the street then came to help with the bags. He picked up three bags then looked at me.

"You should be gettin a beep soon."

"From who?" I questioned.

"Ronnie. She called for you so I gave her ya beeper number."

"Why you do dat?"

"Cause she was lookin for you."

Just as Tone was telling me this, my beeper went off and I checked the number expecting to see an out of town area code but it wasn't. It was a 215. I didn't recognize the number and since I didn't give too many people my number I wondered who it could be. As soon as I got in and put the bags down I called the number and waited for an answer.

"Somebody page Pooh . . ." I asked when a female voice answered the phone.

"Yeah hold on . . ."

"Hello . . ."

"Yeah . . ."

"Who dis . . ."

"It's Ronnie . . ."

"Who . . ."

"Ronnie from Virginia . . ."

"Oh what's up . . ." I said knowing who it was the first time she said it.

"Nothin what's up wit you . . ."

"I'm chillin. Where you at . . ."

"I'm in Philly . . ."

"I know dat. Where at in Philly . . ."

"My girlfriend's house. I drove her up here . . ." "What you doin . . ."

"Nothing. I was kinda hoping that we could get together. I wanna see you . . ."

"I don't know bout dat. I gotta work later . . ."

"On a Saturday . . ."

"Yeah . . ."

"No he don't," Tone yelled as he sat on the sofa next to me.

"Who was that . . ."

"Tone . . ."

"So who's telling the truth . . ." she asked me. "What's you talkin bout . . ."

"He said you don't have to work, you said you do. Who's telling the truth . . ."

I didn't respond to her question. Instead I looked at Tone who was laughing because he knew that he had put me in a tight situation. I stuck my middle finger up at him and all he did was laugh harder causing me to laugh.

"Pooh what's so funny . . ."

"Nothin . . ."

"Are you goin to answer my question or not . . ." "I guess

I could get off work . . ."

"How you gonna do that . . ."

"Tone goin work for me . . ." I told her and he stopped laughing and this time he stuck his middle finger up at me.

"Cool, so what you wanna do . . ."

"We can chill . . ."

"Where you at? I'll meet you . . ."

I immediately knew that this was not a good idea. I did not want her coming to the corner. I thought for a minute of where I could meet her but I must have took too long.

"Did you hear me . . ."

"Yeah, I heard you. I'm tryin to figure out where we can meet . . ."

"Y'all can meet right here," Tone yelled out. "He's right. Tell me where you are . . ." Figuring that her coming here couldn't hurt I gave in. "Ask ya friend if she know where Hancock and Cambria at . . ." I told her and I heard her ask. "She said she know where it's at . . ."

"Dats where I'm at . . ."

"Alright, we'll see you when we get there . . ." "Aiight . . ." I said and hung up the phone.

"Why you do dat yo? I ain't wanna see her?" "Stop lyin. You know you like her."

"I got shit I gotta do today."

"Like what?"

"I gotta work."

"I'm workin for you remember."

Tone had me and he knew it. I was looking for an excuse but he had taken them all away from me and despite what I said out of my mouth I found myself looking forward to seeing Ronnie again. I remembered the last time we were together and had to admit that I had enjoyed it.

"What's up wit Lisette?" Tone asked with a smile on his face and I knew that he had asked me that to be smart.

"Fuck you Tone," I said and he burst out laughing.

The mention of Lisette's name jarred my memory and I remembered that I had to go get the car seat from her sister's house. While agreeing to get with Ronnie I had totally forgotten about that. I looked at Tone thinking about asking him to do it then realized that he was going to work my shift which meant that he wouldn't be able to do it. I struggled to come up with a solution then realized that Lisette had a car now that my CRX was out of the shop.

I called her mom's house and she answered. I told her that I had to cover Mama's shift and that I wouldn't be able to get the car seat from her sister. She asked me could someone else cover until I got back but I told her that I had to do it because Tone had to go somewhere. She whined for a couple seconds then told me that she would go get it herself and hung up.

Rosie who had heard my conversation asked me what was going on and Tone told her everything that was going on including the part about me meeting Ronnie. Rosie simply shook her head and called me an asshole before walking off. I took it in, smiled, then went to the corner to wait for Ronnie.

* * * * *

Over the years the streets taught me a lot of lessons but probably the most painful one I ever had to learn was to not think with my dick. It was nightfall and me and Ronnie were strolling down South Street hand-in-hand like we were a couple. We had been to the movies earlier in the day, then ended up on South Street with me showing her around. We stopped at a steak shop to get something to eat and while we were waiting I decided to turn my beeper back on. I had turned it off while we were in the movie theatre. We were just about to sit down when my beeper began beeping. I checked the number and noticed that it was Tone paging me 911.

Knowing that him paging me 911 meant that he wanted me to call him right back I got up to use the pay phone. Before I could take two steps my beeper went off again with the same page in it. It took me about one minute to get outside to a phone and in that time my beeper went off three more times. I hurriedly put the money in the phone and dialed Rosie's number. Tone answered on the first ring. He instantly asked me where I was at and I told him then he asked me why I hadn't been returning any of his pages. I told him that I had my beeper turned off. I asked him what the emergency was and he told me. It was then that my heart skipped a beat. Before Tone could get anything else out I told him that I was on my way and hung up the phone.

I rushed back inside the steak shop and got Ronnie who looked confused by my rushing. I grabbed her arm and dragged her out of the shop and to my car. I started the car and drove like a mad man back to the block hoping that everything would be alright but preparing to blame myself if it wasn't.

Chapter 11

OCTOBER 1993

The second I stepped into Temple's Hospital emergency room I was rushed by Lisette's family and bombarded with questions of where I had been and why I hadn't been answering my pages. I heard everything that they were saying but couldn't focus on any of it. All I wanted to know was where Lisette was and how she was doing. I tried to ask her mom but she was hysterical and the only thing she wanted to know was where I had been. I was getting nowhere close to finding out how she was doing and this trend would have probably continued had it not been for a doctor emerging from a set of double doors.

Everyone rushed the doctor but to their dismay he was not there to see them. He was there for another family. While everyone's attention was focused on the doctor, Rosie, who had been sitting quietly in a corner, took advantage of the distraction and pulled me by my arm outside to the parking lot.

"Rosie, what's goin. How is she?"

"I don't know yet."

"What happened? All Tone said was that she was in an accident."

"She came to the house not long after you left and she was fine. Mama said she seen her at the corner after she left the house and she looked a little upset then she got in her car and drove off. The cops said she ran a red light at Front and Allegheny and another car ran into her pretty bad."

"How bad?"

"Bunch of cuts and bruises, a couple broken bones and a punctured lung."

"Is she goin make it?"

"They got her in surgery now but um . . ." "What?"

Rosie looked at me like she was struggling within herself on telling me something or not and then it hit me and I hated myself for not asking sooner.

"Da baby?" I asked.

"Um."

"Rosie what about da baby?"

Rosie took a deep breath then looked me straight in my eye. "Dey had to do an emergency delivery because Lisette hit her stomach on the steering wheel in the crash. The baby was hurt and premature and all I know is that they got him on a breathing machine."

"Him. It was a boy?"

"Yeah."

"Pooh ven aca," Lisette's sister said sticking her head out of the door.

I rushed into the emergency room followed by Rosie. When I got to the crowd that was Lisette's family, there was a white doctor standing in front of them explaining the conditions of Lisette and my premature newborn baby. The doctor explained that both Lisette and the baby were in the ICU and that both of them were on respirators. He said that it was very touch and go and couldn't guarantee that either of them would live. My knees buckled as soon as I heard this and I had to grab a nearby countertop to help hold me up.

Rosie noticed my condition and led me over to a chair and sat me down. I sat and listened from a distance as the doctor gave my girl a 50% chance of living and my son a 30% chance. I felt the tears well up in my eyes and as I put my hand up to wipe them I realized that I was too late because they were already rolling down my cheeks. Rosie rubbed the back of my neck and a few seconds later the doctor was gone. I looked up just as Rosie's mom was approaching me. I wiped my eyes and stood up.

"Pooh where were you? We tried to page you for four hours."

"My battery in my beeper was dead."

"Why was she driving the car? I thought you were supposed to go get the car seat then she says that you called and said that you couldn't go get it and that she had to."

"I was working."

"Mira papi we know you sell drugs and we sent someone to your corner but you weren't there."

"I sent him somewhere to take care of something for me," Rosie said saving me from the barrage of questions.

"Who are you?" Lisette's mother asked.

"I'm the person he works for."

"Why did it take him so long to get here?"

"He came as soon as he found out. I sent him to New Jersey and when he came back my nephew told him what happened and he came as soon as he heard."

"Well he still should have gone to get the car seat like he was supposed to," Lisette's mom said and walked away.

"It's my fault Rosie. I called her and told her to go get da car seat because I had to work so I could go out wit another bitch," I said when Lisette's mom was gone and out of earshot.

"It's not your fault," Rosie said but I knew that she was just saying that for my benefit.

"It is. I should have just gone to get the car seat."

"Forget about that for now. Just worry about your girl and your baby," she told me. Then I felt my beeper vibrate.

"I checked the screen and noticed it was Tone that was paging me. Rosie saw me checking and asked who it was.

"It's Tone," I told her.

"Call him and see what he wants," she told me and I walked over to the phone.

Tone answered on the first ring, he asked how Lisette and the baby were doing and I told him what the doctor had said. I then asked him who was watching the corner if he was on the phone with me and he told me that Mama was. Next he asked me what he was supposed to do with Ronnie who I had dropped off there before I came to the hospital. I told him to tell her to tell her girlfriend to come get her. After all of the questions were answered Tone got to the reason for him paging me.

He told me that he had just finished talking to one of our workers named Carlos or Los for short. He told me that Los told him that one of our other workers named Vic had told him that earlier in the day when Lisette was on the corner that he had told her that he had seen me leaving with another chick. This confused me because Tone was not one for "he say she say," so why was he telling me this? I asked him this. He told me that Vic had told Los that he did it because he wanted to fuck Lisette Tone said his reason for telling me was so that I would be on point.

He said that if it was true then it meant that Lisette knew about me being out with Ronnie. He told me that at least with what I knew I would be able to form a plausible lie. I thought about everything Tone had said then came the only question that I really wanted an answer to. The question was, did Tone believe Los. I asked him and he said that he did. I was silent for a second because I had a thought running through my head and I was trying to piece it together. Tone said my name but I told him to wait a minute then it clicked to me.

I recalled Rosie telling me that when Lisette had been at the house that she had been fine. Then I recalled her saying that Mama had seen her after she had left the house and she seemed upset. It was then that it dawned on me that she was upset when Mama seen her. She was upset because she had just seen Vic and he had told her about me leaving with Ronnie.

My blood began to boil and at the same time Tone was calling me through the phone to get my attention. I told him that I was there and then I asked him to check and see if Vic was still on the block.

Tone told me to hold on while he went to check. I could hear him open then shut the front door and finally he was back at the phone telling me that Vic was indeed on the block. By then I was becoming blinded with rage. I told Tone to keep him there and that I was on my way. I hung up the phone, headed straight for the exit and Rosie followed me out and into the parking lot.

"Where you going Pooh?"

"I gotta take care of somethin."

"Right now with your baby and your girl in the hospital?" she asked me as we got to my car.

"I'll be right back."

"Pooh don't do anything stupid."

"I ain't," I said as I got into my car and started it. Rosie backed away as I pulled off.

It only took me ten minutes to reach the block from the hospital. When I got there Vic was leaning on his car talking to one of the neighborhood girls.

Tone who was already on point wasn't too far away and Mama was next to him. I got out of my car with my gun in my hand but I was holding it by the barrel instead of the butt. I walked right up to Vic and called his name.

"Vic what's up," I said.

As soon as he turned his head to see who was speaking to him I smacked him across his face with the gun and he fell to the ground. I knelt down and put my knee into his chest and began to pistol whip him with all the strength I had in my body. Blood spurted from the many open cuts on his face and he began to choke on the blood that was beginning to clog his airway. Tone allowed the pistol beating to go on for about a minute before dragging me off of Vic.

"Da next time you get in my business I'ma kill you pussy," I yelled as Tone and Mama pushed me up the street.

They escorted me to the house. When we got there Tone told me to go in and clean up and made Mama stay with me. We walked in and I was shocked to find Ronnie sitting on the sofa. As shocked as I was to see her I think she was a little more shocked to see me. I had a gun in my right hand and the gun, the knuckles, and fingers on the hand that clutched the gun had blood dripping from them. My shirt had blood on it and there was a little bit of blood spattered on my face. Not to mention that I was sweating and huffing and puffing.

"Oh my god Pooh what happened?" she asked jumping up

from the sofa.

"I'm cool," I said going into the kitchen to clean my face and hands.

I put my gun on the counter and yelled for Mama to bring me a clean shirt. I took off the one that I had on threw it in the trash and it was then that I noticed the throbbing pain in my hand. Two of the fingers on my right hand were swelling and they hurt like a muthafucka.

I washed the blood off of my hand and face and when I was done I turned from the sink to find Ronnie standing there watching me. She looked kind of frightened and I can't say that I blamed her. I mean what girl from the suburbs of Virginia wouldn't be scared in Da Bad Landz with a sight like this before her.

"Pooh what's going on?" she asked me.

"Nothing. Everything aiight."

"It don't look like it."

"It is. Just go back in the living room and chill."

"I don't want to chill. I want you to tell me what's going on."

"I said ain't nothin goin on."

"Pooh I'm not stupid something is going on and I think I

have a right to know if I'm in danger or not."

"You really wanna know what's goin on?" I asked her becoming agitated.

"Yes I do."

"Aiight. I just pistol whipped a nigga dat told my baby mom dat he seen me leaving in a car with you."

"I didn't know you had a baby mom."

"It's a lot of shit you don't know bout me."

"Like what?" she asked as Mama came into the kitchen with a clean shirt for me.

"Thanks Mama."

"Pooh what else don't I know about you?" Ronnie asked but I ignored her.

"Pooh I know you hear me. Answer me."

"Yo leave me da fuck alone right now." I exploded and she shied away from me for a minute but as soon as she realized she was in no immediate danger she came right back with her question.

"I still want an answer Pooh."

"You want an answer. Aiight here's ya answer. I'm not 18.

I'm 15 and I don't work for no construction company. I sell heroin. I got a babymom who is in da hospital cause she was in a accident leaving here and dats probably because she was mad over what da nigga dat I just pistol whipped told her. Her and my son might not live to see tomorrow and if dey don't den I'ma kill da nigga I just pistol whipped. Anything else you want to know?"

Ronnie looked shocked as did Mama. Ronnie was silent for a minute then she looked at me and spoke in a very soft voice.

"Why'd you lie to me?"

I chuckled hearing this and put on the shirt that Mama had given me. I picked up my gun and wiped it off then put it back on my waist. I made sure it was secure then headed for the front door. Ronnie followed me.

"Why'd you lie Pooh?"

"Mama make sure she call her friend and dat dey get out of da neighborhood safely. I'm goin back to da hospital."

I was out the door and down the steps when Ronnie got to the front door and called out after me.

"That's it Pooh. You just goin walk away without answering me?"

"I'll talk to you later," I said without turning around.

MARCH 2001

C.F.C.F UNIT D2-1

"Papi is you listening?"

"Yeah I hear you." I lied. I hadn't heard a word that my son has said.

This was how it usually went on visits when Lisette brought all three of my kids. All three of them talked at once and all three of them demanded that I listen to everything that they said. I did my best but I normally only caught a third of what each of them said but it was enough. I love my kids. They are my world along with Lisette. Without them my life just wouldn't be the same.

My son who is seven is my oldest. Armani Nevins nicknamed Army is truly his father's son. He looks just like me and is even beginning to act like me. I am his world and it can be seen in his eyes when he looks at me. When I speak he looks at me like whatever I am saying just has to be the truth. He's very affectionate towards me but lately

I have noticed that he is shying away from the hugs and kisses, opting for a handshake as our greeting and I respect that. Now when we see each other we exchange firm handshakes but when he is departing I still kiss him on the top of his head which he allows and I appreciate his allowance.

My other two kids are a totally different story.

Yaritza and Maritza, twin girls, age five are true daddy's girls. Whenever they see me all they do is hug and kiss me the entire time that we are together and I love the affection between us. The girls look more like Lisette than me but just like Armani they have most of my characteristics. They are beautiful little girls. One look at them and you can tell that they are Puerto Rican. The only thing that gives away them being mixed is their last name. If not for the them having a name like Nevins you would never suspect that they had black in them. Their hair is already at their shoulders and they have the same light eyes that their mother possesses. Speaking of their mother I must give Lisette the credit that she deserves. She is raising my girls just like I want.

My worst fear for my daughters is someone one day taking advantage of them and Lisette knows this so she does her best to instill her personality in them and it is working. My daughters understand that they are girls and that there are certain places that they should and shouldn't be touched. They also understand that there is only a handful of men whom they should speak with. Last week on a visit Heem tried to speak to them and they both shied away from him. I smiled because I knew that this was Lisette's doing. She is doing her best to mold them into ladies and I commend her on the job that she is doing.

"Papi titi Rosie got me new shoes so I could play baseball

this summer and she said she gonna get me a glove too."

"Papi I wanna play baseball too. Tell Army I can play."

"Me too papi."

I look at all three of my kids and smile listening to them compete for my attention. I look over at Lisette who is as beautiful as ever and she simply smiles a smile that says I'm on my own.

"Everybody can play baseball, okay."

"No dey can't. Dey girls."

"Dey can play if dey want to," I tell my son.

"Thank you papi." both of my daughters say at the same time as both of them jump into my lap hugging and kissing me.

I enjoy the company of my kids for a few more minutes until the visit comes to an end. My girls hug and kiss me numerous times. Then my son extends his hand. I shake it, then pull him into me. I hug him tightly then kiss him on top of his head. When I stand upright Lisette is also standing and we hug. She whispers to me how much she loves me then we share a kiss that is still as passionate as that first kiss we shared in Bottoms Up eight years ago. She tells me that they'll be back next week then she heads to the door that leads out of the prison. I watch them go and before they exit my son turns and waves at me and yells that he loves me. I tell him I love him too and then they are gone. While I am waiting to get strip searched I look at the pictures we took and I think back to a time when I thought that me having a family with Lisette would not be possible. It was during this time when it was questionable whether I would ever see my son or not. It was during this time that I almost fucked everything up. My relationship with Lisette and my newborn son, my future as a hustla and my freedom.

* * * * *

OCTOBER 1993

I was tired, hungry and dirty but then again so was everybody else that had been at the hospital since Lisette had had her accident. Along with me at the hospital were Lisette's mom and dad, her brother and her two sisters. Rosie had been here but had left the night before although she promised to come back later today. Today was to be a great day for everyone because today was the day that Lisette was to come off of her breathing machine. The doctor had come to see us a few hours ago and informed us of this and said that he would be back to let us know how everything went.

My son was a different story. The doctors still weren't comfortable taking him off of the respirator. I had seen him a few days ago and it nearly broke my heart to see him in that condition. He was small and he had all types of tubes running in and out of his body. Because only the mother and father were allowed in the infants ICU, I had to describe his condition to Lisette's family and as soon as I did her mother broke out into tears.

Lisette's doctor finally came walking through the double doors and approached us and we all stood. He spoke a lot of doctor jargon at first but what it all boiled down to was that Lisette was breathing on her own and was doing much better. Her mom asked if they could see her and the doctor said that at the moment she didn't want to see anybody but someone named Pooh.

I looked at him when I heard him say this and he asked me was I Pooh. I told him that I was and he instructed me to follow him. He led me through the double doors and down a corridor to a room that was dimly lit and filled with patients all hooked up to various machines. He pointed Lisette out to me and I made my way over to her bed. Her face was still slightly bruised but other than that she looked fine. I thanked God that she had survived.

"Hey," I said softly as I approached her bedside.

"Hey," she responded.

"How you feelin?" I asked her.

"I hurt a little but it's getting better."

"You had me scared."

"Yeah."

I was picking up her tone and it was as if she wasn't happy to see me. I knew that that had something to do with what Vic had told her.

"Where were you Pooh?" she asked me.

"I been right here in da hospital."

"I mean where were you when I came to da corner dat day?"

"I had to make a run for Rosie." I lied, trying to see if I could convince her that what Vic had told her was a lie.

"Please don't lie to me Pooh."

"I'm not lyin."

"So you didn't get in a car wit another girl?" "No."

"Pooh, if you love me like you say you do, why you lie to me? What you think that if you tell me the truth that I won't understand? We love each other Pooh. We can work through anything as long as we know we telling each other the truth at all times."

I listened to what she was saying and she sounded so sincere that I knew I had to tell her the truth. What I didn't know was that her sounding sincere was just a ploy to get me to admit to what she already knew and I fell for it. I was about to give her enough ammunition to do what she was planning on all along.

"Alight, listen. I was wit another chick but I swear it was nothing."

"It was nothing?"

"Nothing."

"You remember what I told you when we first met Pooh?"

"What?"

"About cheatin on me. I told you I was leavin you if you ever cheated on me."

"But you just said we could work through it."

"I lied, just like you were doing."

"Lisette listen . . ."

"No, you listen Pooh. We're done. I don't wanna see you no more. I don't wanna be with you no more and I don't want you around our son."

"What?"

"You heard me."

"You can't keep me from my son."

"Watch me," she said and pressed a small button.

About a minute later a nurse appeared in the doorway and asked Lisette was everything alright.

"I don't want him in here," she told the nurse and I looked at her like she was crazy.

"What you doin?" I asked her.

"Sir, I'm going to have to ask you to leave," the nurse said but I ignored her.

"Lisette you serious?" I asked but she said nothing. Then out of the blue there were two security guards grabbing me by my arms.

"Get da fuck off me," I yelled and tried to break free but they were too strong.

"Pooh, just go," Lisette said with tears in her eyes.

"I ain't goin no fuckin where," I responded but I was wrong because before I knew it the guards hustled me out of the ICU and back into the lobby where Lisette's family looked at me like I was crazy.

The guards let me go and I thought about swinging at one of them but decided against it because they probably would have fucked me up. Lisette's mom asked me what was going on but I ignored her and stormed away to the elevators. One was opening as I got there and I took it to the bottom floor. When I got off I rushed from the hospital and jumped in my car heading to the block.

While I was stopped at a red light I thought about what Lisette had said to me and I began to blame everybody else for what had happened when in all actuality it was my fault. The person I blamed the most was Vic and while I waited I became more and more upset until I found myself going under my seat for my gun. The light changed to green and I peeled away cursing Vic out in my head for opening his mouth in regards to something that didn't concern him. I drove the rest of the way to the block with one thing on my mind and that was finding Vic. When I look back at the incident now I realize that if Vic hadn't been around when I pulled up, that I probably would have calmed down by the time that I seen him but that wasn't to be the case.

As soon as I pulled up I seen Vic, battered face and ad going into Santos' store. My anger raged at the sight of him. I parked my car, got out with my gun in my hand and walked swiftly to the store. Before entering I saw Mama and she saw me. She called out to me but I ignored her as I entered the store. When I got inside Vic was standing at the counter paying for something. I was getting ready to say something to him but then I remembered what Tone had told me when I had killed the nigga who had stomped my mom.

He told me that when you're about to kill someone you should never talk to them because it gives then a chance to try something. With that in mind and the conversation I had just had with Lisette playing in my head, I raised the gun that I had. As soon as I raised the gun Vic turned towards me but didn't appear frightened, just surprised. He tried to rush me and I fired twice hitting him once. He grabbed his shoulder where I had hit him and before he could try anything else I shot him again in his chest and he fell to the floor. I quickly walked over to him. He put his arms up as if that would prevent what was about to happen. I stood over top of him and I heard Tone telling me to always make sure that the job was finished. I pulled the trigger twice more hitting Vic in his face. I looked up at Santos who was reaching for something under the counter and raised my gun to kill him too but someone grabbed the gun and my arm at the same time.

"Get da fuck . . ." I said as I turned and came face to face with Mama.

"What da fuck is you doin Pooh?"

"He saw me kill Vic."

"So what. Dis is Santo. He ain't goin say nothin. Right Santo?"

"Yo no vi nada."

"Good. Now Pooh give me da gun and get da fuck out of here," she said and I handed her my gun then ran outside.

I jumped in my car and drove off as fast as I could. I drove but I had no idea where I was going. I knew that I had to get off the streets but I didn't know where to go. So for the time being I headed to Rebecca's house because after all that was where Spud hid out after catching his body. As I drove I took notice of something. My hands weren't shaking like they were the first time. I also noticed that it was as simple as Tone and Spud had made it seem. All I had to do was point and squeeze. It was simple but it would get a lot more complicated.

Chapter 12

MARCH 2001

C.F.C.F UNIT D2-1

I am at my sink brushing my teeth when Daniels calls over the blocks intercom that the block is open. Immediately you hear doors opening and people rushing to the showers which there are only eight of on the block. I finish brushing my teeth and grab my laundry bag with my shower gear in it and step out of the cell. Heem is already in one of the showers. He tells me that I'm on him and I nod my head so he knows that I heard him.

I stretch my arms and legs and it feels good. This is the first time that we have been out of our cells in two days because three niggas got stabbed over a beef that is brewing between North Philly and West Philly. As I look around I can see the tension between the warring factions. The North Philly niggas are standing in one area of the dayroom while the West Philly niggas are standing in another. I look at both groups and I am supremely pissed off because they drew so much heat that the shake down crew hit the block and I had to flush my cell phone.

Heem who was also involved gets out of the shower and gets my attention. I walk over to the shower. On my way there I look up at the desk and notice that Daniels is the only guard there. This is unusual because normally there has to be two guards working in order for our block to be open because we have multis. I look on for a second more then get into the shower stall. I take fifteen minutes in the shower then get out cause I know other niggas is waiting to use it. When I get out I look up at the desk to get my door opened and I noticed that there is another c/o at the desk. Me and the other guard lock eyes for a second then I signal for my cell to be opened.

Mi-Mi looks at me then finally opens my cell door and I enter closing it behind me. I haven't seen or spoken to Mi-Mi since my visit with Ronnie which was about two weeks ago. The day of the visit I tried to call her twice but both times I got her voice mail so I left messages which she never returned. The next day I did the same thing and got the same response so I stopped calling altogether.

I lotion up and get dressed then decide to use the block phone since I don't have one of my own anymore. I press the call button and my door opens. I look up to the phones but they are all in use and the line of niggas waiting is about thirty deep. I look at the phones. On the first one is a nigga that Heem is cool with who spends a lot of time around us so I call out to him. When he looks up I ask him who is on him. He points at me and I nod my head. Since he'll probably be on the phone for at least another ten minutes I go sit at one of the tables on the tier where we eat at and wait. I'm sitting there for about five minutes when I look out the window at the front of the block and notice a bunch of new niggas at the bubble on center control. Three of the niggas are directed to come to our block and as they enter the block one of them looks extremely familiar.

As he goes to the desk with the other three new dudes I look at his face. I run through my memory trying to make sure that he's not an enemy. When I'm pretty sure that he's not I try to figure out where I know him from. He is directed to a cell on the top tier. As he turns to head to his cell he locks eyes with me and a smile appears on his face. As soon as he smiles I recognize him. It's Stiz from Germantown. I had met Stiz in '93 when I got locked up for killing Vic. Back then the very first thing you noticed about Stiz was his huge smile and looking at him now I see that hasn't changed too much.

"Pooh what's up baby?" Stiz asks when he sees me.

"Ain't shit," I respond getting up from the table to shake his hand.

"I seen you on da news nigga. Dey tryin to say you killed a cop huh?"

"Yeah but dat shit ain't bout nothin." I lie knowing damn well that my case was definitely about something.

"Damn homie, it's been a long time since I seen you. What you been doin?"

"Chillin. Tryin to get to a dolla. When you come home from upstate?"

"I maxed out like three months ago."

"You just maxed out and you back already?" "Yeah I got caught up in some nut shit."

"You got drama?"

"Yeah, but I ain' t have shit to do wit what dey charged me wit."

"What dey charge you wit?"

"A body."

"You got a lawyer?"

"Hopefully my man get me one like he pose to." I was getting ready to say something else when the phone that I was waiting for opened up. I tell Stiz that I'll talk to him later, then go and get on the phone. I receive a few crooked glances because I bypassed the line but it doesn't mean anything because this type of shit happens all the time. Dudes always bypass the line and every time it happens it is always the same faces waiting in line. To me these dudes are nuts. I wish I would wait in line for the phone only for someone else to walk past me like I wasn't even standing there and grab the phone before me. But hey, if they didn't care then let them wait.

I dial my number and while I wait for someone to answer I turn and catch Mi-Mi looking at me. She looks past me for a second then looks back at me and mouths the words 'I'm sorry.' I give her no kind of response as Lisette answers the phone and we begin to talk. I use all my phone time then walk back to my cell where Heem is waiting on me.

"What's up wit ya chick?" he asks, pointing to Mi-Mi.

"We goin through somethin right now."

"Like what?"

"She think she more important den she is." "Here she come," he says and I notice Mi-Mi walking in our direction. Heem walks off just as she is approaching.

"What's up?" she asks when she reaches me. "Chillin," I respond in a cold tone.

She looks around to make sure that no one is listening to our conversation then focuses back on me. "I tried to call you yesterday."

"I had to flush my phone."

"What you don't feel like talkin or something?" she asks obviously picking up on my vibe.

"I'm aiight."

"Pooh, why is you actin like dis? I said I was sorry."

"I ain't actin like nothin. You da one dat started trippin."

"I know and I said I was sorry."

"And I heard you."

"What I gotta do to make it right between us?" "You gotta know ya place."

"And what my place pose to be?"

"Dig dis Mi-Mi. I fucks wit you but dis is what it is. I'm in jail and more den likely I ain't neva goin home again so we ain't doin nothin but havin a jailhouse thing and if you can't accept dat den you gotta go bout ya business."

"Why you gotta say it like dat?"

"I keep it real sweetheart. I'm goin to jail for a long time and I got two chicks dats goin ride wit me till the wheels fall off and I can't jeopardize dat for you."

"What makes you think I ain't goin ride wit you. I'm ridin now, ain't I?"

"Dats now and dats cause I'm here and you can get wit me but when I get up in dem mountains it's goin be a whole new ball game. You goin find you a new nigga and do ya thing."

"Is dat what you think?"

"Yeah."

"Pooh I can have almost any nigga in da city dat I want but I'm wit you and I know all bout ya case but dat shit don't mean nothin to me."

"If you say so."

"I do."

"We'll see."

"Aye yo Pooh what's up?" Stiz calls as he walks towards me and Mi-Mi.

"I gotta holla at my man."

"Can we finish talkin later?"

"Yeah, we can do dat."

"Okay. Oh, and I know you was goin have to flush ya phone so I brought you another one and a few otha things. I'll get em to you later."

"Aught," I say as she walks away and Stiz approaches.

"Yo, shorty tough as shit," he says.

"She aiight. So what's up wit you nigga?" I ask changing the subject.

"Chillin dog. Yo, you been on da streets since you beat dat body back in da day?"

"Yup, I caught a couple cases but dey was all bullshit."

"Dats whats up. Yo, I still remember dat day you beat dat case you was happy as shit."

"Ain't no doubt," I respond.

Stiz probably remembered that day because he was court with me. I definitely remembered it because it was like the weight of the world was lifted off of my shoulders.

* * * * *

FEBRUARY 1995

February 17th, 1995 was the day that I had been anticipating for thirteen months. Mama who was my codefendant had also been waiting for this day only she had been waiting for three months more than I had. Two days after I killed Vic the Homicide Detectives locked Mama up after hearing that she had been the one who took the gun from me when I fled the store. They didn't really want Mama but they did want the gun. They also wanted to know where I was hiding. She wouldn't give them any information on either topic so they charged her with conspiracy and made her my codefendant.

While I was on the run I learned that she was locked up through Rosie who was in constant contact with me the entire time. Rosie told me that there was nothing that I could do but run until I got caught. She told me that when I got caught she would have a lawyer for me and that I would be well taken care of no matter what happened. I spent the first two days at Rebecca's house until a better arrangement sort of fell into my lap. I was playing with Spud's son when my beeper went off. I looked at the display screen and saw a 703 area code. I had no clue where that was and I was afraid to call back so I got Rebecca to do it. When she found out who it was that was calling she put her hand over the mouthpiece of the phone and told me that it was someone named Ronnie. I debated for a few seconds about whether I should take the call or not until I finally took the phone from Becca.

The very first thing Ronnie asked me was why did I lie to her. I was getting ready to become indignant but then decided against it and I explained to her that I lied because I never thought that I would see her again. She didn't respond when I said that so I told her that I was sorry for lying to her. She accepted my apology and we began to hold a regular conversation. She told me that she really liked me even though I had a girl and a baby. She even asked me if they were okay and I told her that they were getting better. Ronnie told me that she didn't care about how old I was or that I sold drugs. She even went so far as to tell me that she didn't care that I had a girl.

She told me that she liked me and that she was willing to be my girl on the side if I would let her, her only stipulation being that I never lied to her again. When she told me this a light bulb went off in my head. I told her that if she didn't mind then I would love to have her as my side girl. Then I suggested that I come to Virginia to see her. She explained to me that she was knee deep into her school work and that she really didn't have too much free time. I told her that I didn't mind and she told me to come down.

Ronnie was the reason that I was able to stay on the streets three months longer than Mama. I had been in Virginia three days staying at Ronnie's small one bedroom apartment when I took one of the biggest gambles in my life. I told her why I was really in VA. Surprisingly she didn't react like I thought that she would. She shrugged her shoulders and told me that I could hide with her as long as I wanted and I accepted.

This arrangement was great for three months until I made a grave mistake by thinking that I could come back to the city. I figured that after three months of hiding that the search had surely died down. I told Ronnie that I was going to Philly for the weekend and would be back Sunday or Monday night. I wouldn't. I hadn't been in the city for three hours before I was arrested and taken to the Homicide Unit. I didn't answer any of their questions and after a while they got fed up and shipped me to the Youth Study Center on the certified side where I would await my trial as an adult on murder charges. I was hoping that I would get a break like Spud and get charged as a juvenile. The first time that I seen a judge the lawyer that Rosie had hired for me tried to get me that break we were shot down. I thought that this was bad but it only got worse at my preliminary hearing. At my hearing I realized that there was someone else present in Santos' store besides me, Mama, Santos and Vic. There was someone else there who hid when the shooting started and this witness had the potential to bury me. He testified that he saw me enter the store, shoot Vic four times then hand the gun to Mama. When he had finished testifying I looked at my lawyer who didn't look confident at all. I looked back to Tone and Rosie and Tone gave me a look that said don't worry about nothing. I relaxed a little but not much.

As I was turning back to the front of the courtroom I noticed that Lisette wasn't there and truthfully I didn't expect her to be. Since I had been locked up I had been trying to get in contact with her. I had written her and called her all to no avail. I had even gone as far as trying to have Rosie talk to her but that didn't work either. I hadn't spoken to her since that day in the hospital and I now truly believed that it was over between us and was ready to move on. Ronnie had stood by my side the entire time that I had been locked up and I knew that she wasn't going anywhere.

This morning I entered the courtroom after Mama and when I got there she looked just as she had everyday since the trial started. She looked like she didn't have a care in the world. She lightly touched my hand as I walked by her as she had been doing every day since we began fighting this case. It was like this was her way of reassuring me that everything was going to be alright. When I took my seat I turned to look behind me. As usual Rosie and Tone were there but to my surprise there was someone else in attendance and her presence shocked me. Next to Tone was Ronnie who smiled at me and mouthed that she loved me. I smiled back and mouthed that I loved her too. I did love her. It might not have been the way that I loved Lisette but I did love her and she knew it.

Of course my mom wasn't there and through Rosie and Tone I had heard that she gotten worse during my incarceration. I was at the point of not even caring anymore. The feeling was mutual. My mom didn't care about me and I didn't care about her. I now realize what I was too self-centered to realize back then and that is the fact that the drug was what was causing her to act like she was. I understand that now but in 1995 all I knew was that my mom had left me for dead so I was going to do the same to her.

When I sat next to my lawyer that morning he told me that the jury had come to a verdict and that he felt confident that I would be acquitted. Mama's lawyer had told her the same thing. In my mind I was thinking that he should feel confident. He really didn't have to do anything but ask a bunch of people who didn't see me shoot anyone could they positively identify me as the killer and wait for them to say no. The hard work had been done by Tone who had tracked down the eye witness who had moved to Delaware to hide and forced him into changing his testimony. Once that was the done the case was basically open and shut in our favor.

After his encounter with Tone the witness came to the trial got on the stand and changed everything that he said during my preliminary hearing. He said that the detectives had forced him to lie and say that it was me that killed Vic. He testified that the cops told him that they already had a bunch of witnesses but they still needed an eye witness. He also said that they told him that if he did them this favor that they would do one for him when he needed it. The District Attorney did everything they could to get the witness to admit that he had been intimidated but he stuck to his story. It was then that I began to feel confident about my chances at seeing the streets again.

Everyone stood as the judge entered the courtroom, he told everyone to sit. Then he and the lawyers began to have discussions about things I really paid no attention to. These discussions lasted for about fifteen minutes. When they were done the moment of truth came. The judge ordered the jury be brought into the courtroom and I sat up straight preparing to have my fate delivered to me. The judge said a few words to the jury then he asked them if they had reached verdict. The foreman said that they had. The judge asked the foreman to stand. They began reading my charges. After each charge the judge asked the verdict and on all counts the verdict was not guilty. I breathed a huge sigh of relief then shook my lawyers hand. I looked back at Tone and winked and he did the same in return.

The judge thanked then dismissed the jury. Just as he was about to address the court the detective who had worked my case came rushing into the courtroom heading straight to the prosecution's table. He whispered something in her ear and her face turned red. Then she turned and glared at me. The judge noticed the exchange and asked was something wrong. The DA composed herself then informed the judge that she had just been told that the eye witness who had changed his statement was found murdered. He'd been shot four times in the head in an abandoned house in Da Bad Landz. Hearing this the judge too looked at me then informed the DA that there was nothing that he could do. He told her that that was an issue to be taken up with the police then promptly released me and Mama from custody.

* * * * *

As we parked in front of Rosie's house I looked down to the corner and saw that even though it was chilly out people were everywhere. It seemed like Rosie and Tone had managed pretty well without me and Mama and this sort of bothered me. I had been away from the block for sixteen months and I was pretty sure that things had changed. As soon as I got out of the car I took a step towards the corner but Rosie stopped me.

"Don't even think about it. We got some things to talk about," she told me then pointed to the house.

I followed her inside and Tone, Mama and Ronnie followed me. Inside Rosie told me to follow her to the kitchen while everyone else took seats in the living room. As soon as we sat across from each other at the kitchen table Rosie began to chastise me which I knew she had been waiting to do.

"What were you thinking Pooh, killing Vic in the store with all those people around?"

"I don't know Rosie I was trippin."

"For what?"

"Over da shit wit Lisette."

"So you do some dumb shit instead of using your brain?"

"I know and I'm sorry."

"Don't be sorry Pooh. Be smart because now you're going to have the cops breathing down your necks for a while because of the dead witness."

"Now what?" I asked wondering where I stood with her.

"Now we change some things around."

"Like what?"

"Mira Mama, Anthony ven aca," Rosie yelled

into the living room. A few seconds later Tone and Mama entered the kitchen and sat at the table with me and Rosie.

"Like I was just telling Pooh, there are going to be some changes with the block."

"What kind of changes?" Tone questioned. It was obvious that he was in the dark just like me and Mama.

"I'm giving you guys the corner," she said. "What you mean?" I asked her.

"Exactly what I said. Pooh because Tone had to kill the witness on your case it is going to bring a lot of heat down on us heat that I don't want to deal with so I am stepping back. I am going to sell nothing but weight now and that means that the block needs new owners. You three are the new owners."

"Titi we ain't got enough money to run no corner," Tone told her.

"You will. I am going to give you guys the product at the same price that I was getting it at. I'm going to front you the first three re-ups and as long as you run things correctly on the third time you'll have more than enough money to buy from me. The price I will be charging you is cheaper than I will be charging everybody else so keep that to yourselves. The only other thing is that you will have to pay me rent every month which I think is fair since I am giving you guys one of the biggest corners in the city."

All three of us sat there looking at her and personally I was wondering if we could really maintain the corner if it was in our possession. I mean we did good when Rosie was in charge but how would we do on our own. It had never occurred to me that we had actually been running the corner on our own since we took ownership of it when Lefty died.

"Why don't you guys look happy?"

"How much rent?" Tone asked.

Rosie broke down everything to us the prices, the percentages, the rent and when she was done I knew that I had arrived. We all had. The deal that Rosie was offering us was too good to pass on. After breaking everything down to us she told us that we would begin the following Monday. Then she told us that whatever we made between then and now was ours to keep. She said that we could do whatever we wanted with the corner now that it was ours. Her only stipulation being that Teddy's worker stayed put and continued to do what he'd been doing. We agreed.

We all stood up from the table but Rosie stopped me. She told me to sit back down and I did while Tone and Mama went back into the living room to wait for me. When they were gone I looked at Rosie who cocked her head to the side and looked at me for a few seconds before speaking.

"What's going on with you and Lisette?"

"I don't know. I ain't spoke to her since the day I killed Vic."

"Not even once?"

"Nope."

"Alright then listen to me now. You reach out to her once and if she doesn't accept, then you say fuck her and that baby and move on with your life. You never kiss her ass to see your son. That's not right. No man should have to go through that."

I didn't say anything but I shook my head letting her know that I understood what she was saying. I did understand and I agreed with her. I had just spent the last thirteen months wondering if I was ever going to see the streets again. Not once had I heard an encouraging word from the woman who was supposed to love me. I was definitely going to reach out to her but it was going to be when I was ready and not a minute sooner. Me and Rosie spoke for a few minutes more then I got up from the table heading into the living room. I looked at Tone and Mama and we all smiled knowing that our time was now. I was 17 and an owner of Hancock and Cambria.

Tone and Mama stood up from the sofa as did Ronnie. I told her that I had some business to take care of but that she should wait here for me and she sat back down. Tone led the way out of the door with me and Mama following him out of the house and down to the corner.

When we got to the corner people began to callout my name and come up to me welcoming me home. The way that people approached me and spoke to me it was as if my status had went through the roof and it had. I had killed someone and this time it wasn't like the last where it was just a rumor. This time it was verifiable because of the way that it had happened. I was now a force to be reckoned with in the hood and I would be treated as such from that day forward.

All of the workers greeted me with handshakes then the females began to greet me with hugs and kisses. Some were even so bold that they grabbed my dick and whispered to me that they had welcome home presents for me. Once all of this was done I looked around at everything that was going on and realized that it was now partially mine. If the day that Spud killed the man that killed Cuba changed our lives forever then this day definitely cemented our fate.

Chapter 13

APRIL 2001

C.F.C.F UNIT D2-1

A lot of things have changed in the last month. The biggest change is that Mi-Mi is now along with Daniels our everyday guard and things are once again going good between us. She is back to bringing me in whatever I ask for whenever I ask for it. Also once a week she still makes it possible for us to fuck in the school building on the day that they have the religious service. After we had our little talk Mi-Mi stopped acting like a nut about Ronnie coming to see me and agreed to worry only about me and her. Two days later she was working the block again. It was then that she told me that she would be working the block on a regular. When I told Heem about this he commented that she had to be on my dick because if she wasn't she would have never agreed to work a block on a daily basis.

Speaking of Heem that is another change that has occurred. Stiz is now walkie by default. The North Philly, West Philly thing escalated again one day while I was on a visit and when I got back the block was locked down. When I got in my cell my celly told me that Heem and one of the West Philly niggas had stabbed each other real bad on the top tier. He said that the West Philly nigga was taken off the block on a stretcher. He told me that Heem walked to the front of the block before collapsing and they had to call a stretcher for him too.

I missed my homie. Stiz is alright but he is too friendly and at times talks way too much. Basically he doesn't know how to bid like I'm used to. I overlook his shortcomings because I've known him for a while and we have always been cool but sometimes he can be a pain in my ass. The one thing I do respect about him is that he stays on top of his case. He is always on an official visit and always in the law library doing his best to stay on top of what is a fight for his life.

Speaking of fighting for ones life, I got an offer from the DA through my lawyer the other day which I immediately turned down after cursing my lawyer out for bringing it to me. The DA tried to guarantee me life if I testified on Tone and Spud. I wish the fuck I would. I've already resigned myself to the fact that I'm going to jail and I'm fully prepared. I've had a few people ask me how I could say something like that. I just shrug my shoulders as if it doesn't matter and the truth is that it doesn't. Nothing short of a miracle could help me get from under this case.

The crazy part is that we still don't know who put that undercover cop onto us. Now that I am speaking to Tone and Spud again we have been racking our brains trying to figure out who was the one that set us up. When we come up with a possible culprit we also come up with excuses as to why it couldn't have been who we were discussing at that time. One thing I have finally gotten them to agree on is that we got too greedy. When we first got Hancock and Cambria from Rosie everything was good but we made certain moves that slowly but surely would lead to our demise.

* * * * *

MARCH 1995

I took a deep breath as I got out of the car and headed across the street to the third house from the corner. I had enjoyed my first two weeks home to the fullest. I got high, fucked a few bitches and most importantly I along with Tone and Mama got down to the business of running our corner. All of that was great but there was still one thing that I had to do. As I reached the steps that led to the porch and ultimately the front door of the house I was as nervous as ever.

I knew that there were only three people in the house and that was because I had an inside source that had been feeding me information as a favor. I stepped to the door, knocked on it three times then heard the shuffling of feet and the clicking of locks being undone. The door opened and Cookie; Lisette's sister gave me a half smile.

"What's up Pooh?"

"I'm chillin. She here?"

"Yeah, but do me a favor don't tell her I told you to come okay?"

"I won't."

"Alright hold on," she said and closed the door.

I could hear her yelling to Lisette that someone was at the door for her and my heart began to beat faster while I waited for her. I once again heard the shuffling of feet again but this time I also heard something else. It only took me a few seconds to figure out that the gibberish that I was hearing was my son. I listened to him babble until the door swung open. I got a quick glimpse of him before Lisette stepped into my line of sight. We locked eyes for a few seconds, then she broke the stare down and looked towards the floor.

"What you doin here Pooh?"

"I came to talk to you."

"Talk to me about what? You already know how I feel."

"You still trippin off dat?"

"Yes I'm trippin. You cheated on me and I was in an accident because of dat. I almost died Pooh and so did your son."

"Yo, I know I fucked up but what you want me to do? All I can say is dat I'm sorry."

"I warned you Pooh when we first got together what would happen if you cheated on me and you did it anyway."

"Lisette listen, I know I fucked up. I wish I could take it back but I can't so all I can do is apologize. We got a son dat need his dad. He goin be seventeen months old and I neva seen him. What kind of nut shit is dat? I can understand you mad at me but he shouldn't suffer because of dat." Lisette just stood there looking at me like what I was saying was going in one ear and out the other. For the first time since I had known her I became fed up. I had said I was sorry more times than I could count. I had been apologizing for close to a year and a half and still she was acting like a sucka. I was fed up with it.

"You know what man. Fuck it. Do whateva you wanna do. I don't even care no more," I said as I turned and walked down the steps to the pavement.

"Pooh where you goin?" she asked me just as I was about to step off of the curb.

"I'm leavin. I ain't got time to sit here and beg you to see my son. I got otha shit dat I need to be doin."

"Dat otha shit more important den ya family?"

"What family?" I yelled as I turned around. "I ain't got no family except Rosie, Tone and Mama."

"Is dat how you feel?"

"How da fuck else should I feel? I just sat in jail for thirteen months fighting for my life and those was the only muthafuckas dat was there for me."

"So what you sayin?"

"What I'm sayin? I ain't sayin shit. You already said it so dats what it is," I said, turned and headed for my car.

"Pooh," she called out to me but I flagged her and kept walking.

I was putting the key into my door to unlock it when I heard her running up behind me. I spun around just as she was approaching me. She stopped when we were only inches apart and looked up into my eyes. Neither of us said anything we just looked at each other. It was cold and she was barefoot but she stood still as a statue as a solitary tear made its way down her cheek. She reached up and wiped it away but more fell.

"Pooh I'm sorry. I know it's been wrong for me to keep your son from your but I didn't know what else to do. It hurt so bad when I found out that you were with another girl dat I just wanted to hurt you."

"By keeping me from my son?"

"I know it was wrong and I'm sorry. It's just dat you're the first guy dats not my dad or brother dat I eva loved and it broke my heart to know dat you were with someone else."

I didn't say anything. I just stood there looking at her with no makeup on, her hair in a mess and the tears rolling down her face. Regardless of what condition she was in she was still beautiful. She reached for my hand but I flinched and pulled it back.

"Pooh, I'm sorry. Please forgive me," she pleaded and I knew that I wasn't going to be able to resist her even though I wanted to.

I wanted her to feel like I had been feeling since the day that I killed Vic but that wouldn't happen. She took a half-step forward and her head was on my chest. Just the feeling of her body against mine did the trick. I wrapped my arms around her shoulders and she wrapped her arms around my waist tightly.

"Pooh I'm so sorry for actin like I did. I love you."

"I love you too," I responded.

"Come wit me," she said breaking our embrace and pulling me by the hand to the house.

I allowed her to lead me into the house. As soon as we

entered there he was standing in the middle of the living room floor with a stuffed lion in his hand. As soon as he saw me he smiled and ran in my direction with his arms wide open. I scooped him up. He wrapped his arms around my neck and it was the best feeling in the world. I had waited seventeen months for this. I was finally seeing my son. I kissed him on his chubby cheeks and he kissed me back.

"His name is Armani," Lisette told me.

"I know," I responded.

"How?"

I didn't respond this time. Instead I just nodded to her sister who smiled and looked away. Lisette smiled along with her then rubbed our sons head and he turned to his mother.

"Who's dis Army?" she asked him and pointed at me.

"Papi," he told her and my heart melted.

This was the first time that I had ever seen my son and he knew who I was. Lisette told me that she had been talking to him and making him aware of who I was since he was old enough to understand. She said that everyday she pointed to a picture of me and told him that I was his dad and I was grateful for this.

After I had spent an hour with my son I told Lisette that we needed to talk. Her sister agreed to watch Army while we went up to her room to discuss a few things. The first thing that I told her was that I wasn't the same dude that I was before I caught my case. I told her that the stakes were higher for me now. I told her that the next time she did some shit like she had just done to me that is was over for good. She told me that she understood and then she swore to me that she would never do anything like that ever again.

The next topic of conversation was about why she had not contacted me while I was locked up. Before responding she apologized profusely then explained to me that at first she didn't contact me because she was mad. She said that after she got over her initial anger she wanted to write me but she didn't know what to say. I told her that that was a bullshit excuse but if she was willing to forgive and forget that I had cheated on her then I was willing to do the same in regards to her actions. We both agreed to put everything behind us and finally it was time for me to find out the one thing I needed to know. I asked Lisette who she had been messing with while we weren't speaking and she told me nobody.

I looked at her skeptically and she told me again that she hadn't been messing with anybody. She told me that once she got over her initial wave of anger that she realized that she still loved me and wanted to be with me. She said that the thought of having someone else never even crossed her mind and I wanted to believe her. I think that she could sense this and told me that since she first started liking guys that she had only been with three guys and I was the third. At the time I wasn't sure if

I believed her but I knew that I wanted to.

I ended up spending the night as Lisette's that night. Her family was happy to see me and even happier that we had gotten back together. We fucked that night for the first time in over a year and afterwards we fell asleep with our son in between us. It was a great night for me. The next morning when I left I was in the right frame of mind and ready to run the biggest corner in Da Bad Landz.

* * * * *

JUNE 1995

I could see the commotion at the corner as I came out-of Rosie's house. Mama had sent someone up the street to come get me and Tone but Tone wasn't around. I hurriedly walked to the corner and made my way through the crowd where two black guys were arguing with two of my workers and Mama. I made my way to the center of everything and as soon as I did my workers stopped talking.

"What da fuck is goin on?" I asked Mama.

"Da fuckin poppy's tryin to jerk us. Dats what da fuck is goin on," one of the black guys responded.

"I ain't talkin to you," I told him then turned back to Mama.

"Que paso Mama?"

"El moyo esta dijiendo que el tipo lo quemo." "Tu estaba aqui cuando paso."

"Yo, speak fuckin English so we know what y'all talkin bout," one of the black guys said.

I ignored the statement and kept talking to Mama. So far all I had learned from her was that the black guy was accusing one of my workers of burning him for something. I didn't know what yet but I was trying to get to the bottom of it. I asked Mama was she there when it happened and she said no.

"What happened?" I asked the most vocal black guy as I turned to face him.

"Poppy tried to burn me for my fuckin bread," he said.

"Stop wit da poppy shit."

"Man fuck all dat. I'ma say what I want." "Fam I'm tryin to get to da bottom of dis so let's talk sensible. Which one you talkin bout?"

"Him," he said and pointed to one of my case workers named Joel.

I looked at Joel whose face remained impassive. "Joel what happened?" I asked him.

"I don't know what he talkin bout."

"My worker said he don't know what you talkin bout," I

told the black guy as I turned back to him.

"Dat nigga da fuck lyin. He know what da fuck I'm talkin bout."

"Yo, let's chill wit all da cursin and disrespect."

"Fuck dat. I ain't doin no chillin. I want my money or my product."

"You goin chill or it's goin be a problem."

The black guy was getting ready to say something else when his smarter and more observant associate calmed him down. I had bean watching this associate out of the corner of my eye the entire time and all he had been doing was looking at the number of people that had them surrounded. He wasn't stupid. He knew that if his loud mouth homie kept up with his tirade that it wouldn't end good for them. Instead of letting it reach this level he stopped his homie from going overboard and stepped up to speak to me.

"Yo, check dis out. We don't want no trouble. We just want what's ours."

"And what's dat?"

"He tried to short us. We paid for ten racks and he only gave us six."

"Dey only gave me enough for six," Joel said in his own

defense.

I remained silent for a minute while I decided what to do. We had owned the corner for three months now and we were trying to build a reputation as good businessmen apart from what we had done with Rosie. I knew that this would be a good chance to show people that Hancock and Cambria did good business and I intended on doing that.

"Dale el material y los chabo patra," I told Joel.

"Pero Pooh ello estan mintiendo," he said telling me that the two black guys were lying.

"Advanca y alo."

I walked out of the crowd and watched as Joel gave the black guys their product and their money back which was what I had instructed him to do. Once the guys had gotten everything, they got in their car but before pulling off, the smarter more calmer of the two looked at me and nodded his head. I nodded back and they pulled off. A few minutes later business was back to normal and the little scene that had just played out was forgotten by most everybody except me. This was not the first time that something questionable had transpired with Joel at the center of it. There had been an instance when some money had come up short and Joel had blamed it on one of the other workers. The worker Joel claimed was at fault denied everything at first but when I had him and Joel face-to-face he changed his story and admitted to keeping some of the money. I found this strange because the worker didn't seem to be doing it because he knew that he had been caught red handed. It was more like he was scared. Since he had admitted to the discrepancy there was nothing that I could do but I knew something wasn't right.

Just like I knew that something wasn't right then, I knew something wasn't right with this situation. I looked at Joel who continued on like nothing had happened and for some reason I knew that he was getting over on us. I didn't have any proof but then I realized that I didn't need any. This was my corner and I could do anything that I wanted to. I was getting ready to get up and approach Joel when I heard the call letting everyone know that the police were coming.

"Bahando," the young lookout named Bebe called out loud enough for everyone to hear.

I watched the cops cruise down Cambria Street and when they were gone I looked at Bebe and nodded to him letting him know that he was doing a good job. I had recently hired Bebe despite the reservations that Tone had about the wild teenager. I had been watching Bebe and his antics since I had come home from beating my homicide. While I disapproved of most of the shit that he did I had still taken a liking to the young nigga.

He had tremendous downside which was why Tone had objected to me hiring him but I was willing to deal with his downsides of which there were many. First and foremost he was a troublemaker. He was always doing something to something or someone. There were always stories of him stealing something or breaking something and there was even the occasional story of him doing some weird shit like setting a cat or dog on fire. He was annoying and he didn't care how many times someone threatened to fuck him up for doing something. If he felt like doing it again he was going to do it and there was nothing anyone could do about it.

This was one of the main reasons that I was willing to deal with Bebe's downsides. In my mind his upside was what people should have been focusing on. The kid had the heart of a lion and his actions were testament to that. I also seen loyalty in him whereas other people only saw a bad little nigga. I remember the day that I talked to Bebe for the first time. After that conversation I knew that this was going to be my first official young bul.

During this conversation I learned that like me Bebe had a dope fiend for a mom and that he was basically fending for himself. While we were talking I noticed that his usual "I don't give a fuck" attitude had disappeared and was replaced with a much more subdued one. Through that conversation with Bebe I learned that me and him had a lot in common. We were both sons of junkies. We both had no father and we were both only children. We talked for about an hour that day and when I got up off the steps that we were sitting on I found myself asking Bebe if he wanted to work for me. He said that he did and I hired him as my new lookout.

That was two months ago and since the first day that he had worked on the block everyone had noticed a drastic change in him. He no longer ran around the hood doing dumb shit. He didn't cause any trouble. In fact he barely did anything but hang on the block. He did this even when he wasn't working. Everyday I made it a point to spend at least a few minutes with him and during these conversations it always seemed as if he had matured a little more. He was my young bul and he knew it. He knew that I was fond of him and he also knew that among the workers that he was the closest to me even if we had only know each other for two months.

"Bahando." Another call signaling the presence of the cops came and this time the cops were on Hancock street.

Once they were gone I signaled Bebe over to me and he made his way to the steps where I was sitting. This was going to be another test. Over the past two months I had put him through a few different tests and he always passed. I had once left him in my car with a lot of money in plain sight and he never touched it. Another time I overpaid him on purpose and within minutes he had returned the extra money telling me that I had given him too much. Time and time again he showed me that he was honest but now he would have to prove that he was loyal.

I shook his hand as he approached then motioned for him to sit next to me and he did. I yelled to Mama for her to look out for the cops for a minute. She said okay then I got down to business with Bebe.

"What happened earlier?" I asked him.

"Wit what?"

"Wit Joel and da moyos."

Bebe didn't respond immediately and I knew that this meant that he knew something. I didn't want him to feel like he was snitching but I also wanted him to understand that this was bigger than whatever Joel had done. This was how we made our living.

"What happened Bebe?"

"Pooh I don't wanna put nobody in trouble."

"Who you work for yo?" I asked him.

"What you mean?" he asked me confusingly.

"I mean who you work for?"

"You."

"Right so when I ask a question bout somethin dat happened on my corner I expect my worker to give me an answer. It ain't bout you gettin nobody in trouble. It's bout you bein loyal to da nigga dats goin be loyal to you."

Bebe put his head down and looked at his feet. He fidgeted

and while he was doing all of this I lit a cigarette. I could tell he was struggling with his decision. I didn't want to pressure him into doing the right thing. I wanted him to do it on his own. There was noise and confusion surrounding us everywhere but between us there was silence for about two minutes, then he spoke.

"Pooh I don't want to snitch on nobody."

"Dis ain't snitchin . . ." I started but he cut me off.

"If I tell you what happened behind his back it is snitchin. So I gotta tell you what happened in front of him."

I looked at Bebe and smiled. The young bul was smart and I loved his smarts. I told him that if that was the way he wanted to do it then we would do it that way. I stood to call Joel just as Tone pulled up in front of me playing Spanish Reggae. He hopped out of his car and hugged me and shook Bebe's hand. I took a few seconds to explain to him what was going on and what was about to happen and he told me to call Joel over. Right before I called out to him Bebe corrected Tone. He told me to call over Joel and the other worker that had been there when we were arguing with the black guys.

I called Joel and the worker who was named Loco and our soon to be former employees made their way over to us. Joel walked with a cocky gait and from what I had heard about him he earned the right to walk like that. Joel was 20 and had been establishing quite a name for himself over the last few years. I didn't know him before I got locked up but I had heard about him. He wasn't from our hood. He was from 5th and Westmoreland but he hung in our hood a lot. This was how he had come in contact with Tone and ended up being my replacement while I was locked up.

"What's up?" he asked as he reached us.

"Go head Bebe," I told him.

"Joel, did gag da moyos. I heard him and Loco talkin bout it when dey was goin to get the dope."

"What? Pooh, he lyin," Joel said.

"Shut up," I told him.

"You sure Bebe?"

"Positive."

"Y'all fired," I said looking at Joel and Loco.

"Fired for what. He lyin."

"I believe him more den I do you so you fired."

"Get da fuck outta here. Tone tell dis nigga something," Joel said.

"I ain't telling him nothin. He said you fired, so you fired."

"Dis bullshit. Y'all ain't really got no power. Y'all shouldn't even have this corner. Y'all only got it cause Teddy killed Lefty and people know he got parts in da block. If he didn't, y'all would have been out of business."

SLAP, SLAP.

The two slaps were lightning fast and loud enough to catch the attention of anybody within thirty feet of us. Joel grabbed his cheek which was starting to bruise with a shocked look on his face. Tone clenched his fists, he had a look on his face like he dared Joel to try something.

"Dats what you get you pussy for runnin ya fuckin mouth. You talkin shit you don't know nothin about. We run dis corner and don't nobody try nothin cause dey know me and my homie ain't goin for it. Everybody know who Tone and Pooh is and now you know too. Now get da fuck off our corner," Tone told Joel who was still holding his cheek.

Joel had a look of murder in his eyes. He must not have had a gun on him cause from what I had heard about him he was quick to pull the trigger. With no gun he just stood there holding his cheek, obviously not wanting any part of Tone in a fight. After holding his cheek for about thirty seconds he turned and walked to the corner and disappeared on Cambria Street with Loco trailing behind him.

"Dats how you handle pussies," Tone said once they were gone.

I looked at Bebe who looked as if nothing had happened. "You ready to hustle?" I asked him.

"Yeah," he responded.

"Good. Finish Loco's shift today and work it from now on."

Bebe simply nodded his head and headed to the corner to get to work. I watched him go and my affinity for him grew even more after what had just transpired. Later on that night it would grow even more because he would save my life.

* * * * *

Had it not been for Rosie, me and Tone would have slept through the knocking on the front door. After the incident with Joel, me and Tone went to Rosie's house where after smoking a few blunts we both fell asleep.

"Answer the fucking door," Rosie yelled from the kitchen loudly.

I slowly opened my eyes and let them adjust to the light that was on above me. I sat up on the sofa and looked over at Tone who was curled up on the much smaller love seat. I chuckled at the uncomfortable looking position that he was in. The knocking resumed and Rosie yelled for one of us to open the door again so

I got up off of the sofa and went to the door.

"What's up Bebe?" I asked when I opened the door and noticed him standing on the steps.

"I need to tell you something."

"Come in," I said as I stood to the side to allow him in.

"What you need to tell me?"

"Joel and four other guys is sittin in a car on da corner."

"How long dey been there?"

"Like five minutes."

"Tone get up," I called out to him but he didn't stir. "Tone." I practically yelled this time and he rolled over. "Yo, wake up."

"What nigga I'm tired."

"Get up. We might have a problem."

"What nigga?" Tone said as he sat up and rubbed his eyes.

"Bebe said Joel and four niggas is sittin in a car on da corner."

"So what. Let em sit there."

"What if dem niggas is waitin on us?"

Tone swung his neck from left to right cracking it, then

stood up and sighed. He went upstairs for about five minutes then came back down with a bag in his hand. He sat back on the love seat and began to empty the contents of the bag onto the table in front of him. Inside the bag there were five handguns. He checked to make sure that all of them were in working order then he handed me one of them. Just as he was giving it to me Mama appeared from out of the kitchen.

"What's goin on?" she asked seeing the guns.

"We might have a problem."

"What kind of problem?"

I told her about Joel being on the corner withsome niggas in a car and she went to the base of the steps and began putting her Timberlands on. When she had tied them she stood and walked over to Tone sticking her hand out.

"What?" he asked her.

"Gimmie a gun."

Tone must have knew that she was serious because he said nothing. He handed her one of the guns then stood and put the other two on his waist.

"Bebe what kind of car dey in?" Tone asked.

"A black Camry. Dey parked on Cambria, across da street from Santos."

"Mama go around the corner and get behind da car. Don't start shooting unless it get crazy. We goin wait in here a few minutes till you get there," Tone told her.

Mama said nothing. She just exited the house. When she was gone Tone told Bebe to stay in the house. Bebe asked could he come but Tone wouldn't let him. We waited a few minutes like Tone said we would then we exited the house and headed for the corner. Halfway there we could see the car and Joel behind the wheel. We were about ten feet from the corner when Joel opened his car door. He was about to get out when I heard someone else in the car tell him to wait.

Joel and whoever told him to wait had a few words that I couldn't decipher. Then Joel closed his door and the back driver's side door opened. I could see Mama behind the man waiting for him to try something but he didn't. He got out of the car and turned, locking eyes with me and I froze. I looked into the eyes of a man I knew but didn't know. I had only seen him twice before in my life. The last time being when I was eleven. Here he was now and no matter hog long it had been I would never forget the face. My father looked at me a few seconds longer then began walking towards me.

Chapter 14

JUNE 1995

From the time that I was old enough to understand the full meaning of the word hate, I knew that the word described how I felt about my father. My mom always told me to never say that I hated anybody but I can't help it. When I was just a baby my in and out of jail junkie father abused my mom physically and mentally until she finally sought refuge in the drug that would ultimately ruin her life. I truly hate this nigga.

I hate him for leaving us. I hate him for pushing my mom into drug addiction with his treatment and I truly hate that he managed to kick the habit while my mom only got worse. During one of his many trips back to one of the numerous state jails that he has frequented he managed to give up the heroin for good and that pisses me off.

My mom keeps getting worse every couple of months hitting a new low while this nigga is now clean without the worries of the heroin monkey on his back. I had heard from one of my aunts that he had recently come home and that he wanted to see me but I declined. I knew that if we saw one another that there was a good chance that we would come to blows and that was a battle I wasn't sure that I could win.

No matter what I felt for him and what he had been into there was one thing that anyone who knew Jose Ortiz would tell you about him. He was a gangsta. Not many people knew that he was my father and that is the way that I wanted it but when I hear people talk about him it is very clear that they fear him. They speak of him with such respect in their voices that you would think he was in their presence when in all actuality he would be in jail somewhere. This was my father, a jailbird, ex-junkie who struck fear in people's hearts and here he was walking in my direction.

The closer he got the more my blood began to boil and before Tone could ask me why me and Jose were looking at one another like that I turned and headed back up the street.

"Darnell wait a minute," Jose called out to me but I ignored him. "Darnell just wait a minute mijo."

Hearing him call me that, I stopped in my tracks and turned to face him. "Don't fuckin call me dat."

"Why not? You are my son right?"

"Fuck no. I ain't ya son and you ain't my dad. You just

some nigga dat got my mom pregnant."

"Listen you right to be mad but dis is important. I'm tryin to help you."

"Help me how?"

"I'm tryin to save ya life. It's three guys in that car just waiting to kill you."

"Ain't nobody killin him," Tone said and quickly came to stand by my side.

"And who you?" Jose asked Tone.

"Da one who goin make sure dat don't nobody kill him."

"Darnell listen to me. Whoeva smacked Joel didn't know who dey were dealin with. We came here to kill you and ya friend. Da only reason dat you're still alive is because I seen you and told them who you are. I got you a pass but you're goin to have to make it right with Joel."

"So if I make it right I get a pass. What about my homie?"

"I don't know nothin bout him. I'm only speakin for you cause I'm ya dad."

"It's cool. Yo fuck dem niggas I ain't makin shit right."

"Son listen . . ."

"Yo stop fuckin callin me dat. I ain't ya fuckin son. Fuck you and dem niggas in dat car. If y'all want problems den so be it. Othawise get da fuck off of my corner and stay da fuck out my face."

I looked at Jose and watched his facial expression change. His eyes grew cold and it could be seen that he didn't like the way that I was talking to him. He took a deep breath then smiled.

"Darnell listen. I know you don't know who I really am so I'm gonna act like you didn't just talk to me like you did but from now on talk to me with some respect."

"Respect for what. Why da fuck should I respect you?"

"Because I earned it. Maybe not as a father but in these streets I earned da respect I demand."

"Nigga fuck you and dat respect shit you talkin," I told him. Tone tried to grab me and lead me away from Jose but I had waited too long to say what I wanted to say and pulled away.

"You don't deserve no respect. You ain't nothin but an ex-junkie. I ain't neva goin respect you. Matter of fact you can suck my . . ."

"SLAP!" I never got the chance to finish my sentence because Jose slapped blood in my mouth.

"How bout now I bet you respect me now you little bitch."

I saw Tone advancing on Jose but there was no way I was going to let him steal this moment from me. Jose noticed Tone too and took his eyes off of me. I spit a glob of blood into the trash can next to me and drew the pistol that Tone had given me. Just as Jose and Tone were about to square off I fired four shots, all of them hitting Jose in his chest. He fell to the ground but he was still alive so I went and stood over top of him.

"You ain't so tough now is you, you fuckin pussy?" I asked as I watched him struggle to breathe.

"Oh shit!" I heard Tone yell. Then gunshots erupted all around me.

The sound of gunfire brought me back to reality and I quickly shot Jose in his face. A bullet grazed my arm and I looked around to find Tone firing both of the guns that he held simultaneously. I watched as Joel crumbled to the ground after taking a slug from one of Tone's guns. Another man who had gotten out of the rear driver's side door also fell victim to Tone. The man in the passenger's seat was shot twice in the back and once in the back of the head by Mama who he never saw coming.

There was people everywhere running for cover and the noise was at an extreme level but somehow we managed to hear one of the lookouts yell "Bahando." Mama came running towards us screaming that the cops were turning off of 2nd

Street. She ran right past us and we followed her. We took a few shortcuts and when we stopped we were out of breath but we were also three blocks from the crime scene. We all tossed our guns in the sewer and went separate ways.

I had only been home four months and already I

was on the run again. We had just killed four people in front of too many witnesses to count or so I thought. We had actually only killed three people. We would learn the next day that Joel had lived. We would also learn that there were no witnesses, well at least none that would identify us or testify against us. After the killing of the witness on my last case the people who might have seen something wanted no parts of telling. They valued their lives too much.

We would get picked up by the detectives but that would be about it. We would never be charged for the case but it would be one of the reasons that the cops of Philadelphia began to focus on us a little more closely. This event would also lead to one of the saddest days of my life.

MAY 2001

C.F.C.F UNIT D2-1

I am sitting on my bed when I hear my cell door open. I look up and Mi-Mi is smiling at me as she pokes her head into my cell.

"Did ya lawyer take care of business?"

"I hope so. He pose to come see me tonight and let me know what's up."

"Well, I took care of everything on my end."

"What ya pop say?"

"Nothin. I'm daddy's little girl. He don't ask me no questions."

"What would you have told him if he did ask you a question?"

"Da truth. I don't lie to my dad."

"Neva?"

"Neva. I don't lie to none of da men dat I love," she says with a sexy and suggestive smile. "I gotta finish my tour. Come holla at me later," she tells me and walks away.

As soon as she leaves, Daniels calls my name over the intercom. I stick my head out of my cell and she tells me that I have a visit. I ask her whether it's an official or regular visit and she says it's official. Bingo. This is what I have been waiting for. I quickly dress and head out.

Ever since I have begun talking to Spud and Tone again we have been trying to get to the same county jail. I talked to my lawyer one day and he said that the DA had requested we all be separated from each other and that the judge had agreed. I asked him was there anything that could be done about this and he told me that from a legal standpoint we were screwed but from a monetary standpoint there were a few things that could be done. I asked him what these things were and he explained them to me. The first two options he told me were not guarantees. The first was that we could bribe two guards to request that Tone and Spud be moved out of their respective jails.

The second option was that we bribe someone high up in the Department of Corrections hierarchy. He informed me that both of these options were easy to execute but that they were not guarantees. He said that with either one of those options a judge could always undo everything and transfer them back to where they came from.

I asked him was there an option that was guaranteed and he told me that there was but that it was more expensive than either of the other two options. He informed me that one of his partners in his law firm was good friends with the judge and that for twenty thousand dollars what I was requesting could be arranged. He explained that this money would buy us a court order from our judge ordering us all placed in the same county jail. As soon as I heard this I asked how much it would cost us to buy our freedom but was informed that that would never happen. I would just have to settle for the presence of my brothers.

"Darnell how are you?" my lawyer asks as I enter the official visiting room.

"I'll be great if you give me some good news."

"Then prepare to be great," he says and slides a piece of paper across the table to me.

I look at the paper and it is an order from the judge stating that me and my co-defendants are to be placed in the same county jail. I examine the paper for a few seconds after the initial reading then slide it back across the table to him.

"I can't tell you what jail you guys will be at but wherever you end up it will happen tomorrow."

"We'll be here."

"How do you know?"

"Trust me I know. Let me ask you dis. What reason did da judge give da DA?"

"He didn't really give a reason. He more or less told the DA that he agreed with the motion that I submitted and that was it."

The motion that he was talking about was one that he filed along with Tone and Spud's lawyers. It requested that we all be placed in the same jail so that we could work together on what defense we wanted our lawyers to use. The motion was nothing more than a sham. It's whole purpose was so that the judge would have a reason to support his action.

I speak with my lawyer for a while longer then I head back to the block. As soon as I return Mi-Mi tells me that I have a regular visit. This surprises me because I'm not expecting a visit today. Mi-Mi hands me my pass and I head back to the visiting room. I change into the orange jumpsuit. Then I'm taken in to wait on my visit which arrives about two minutes after I do. I watch Bebe as he hands the guard his slip. When he walks over we hug and sit down.

"What's up? Why you ain't tell me you was comin?" I ask him.

"I was at a bitch crib up here so I came to see you."

"Dats what's up. How shit runnin?" "Everything is good. I collected all da money dat niggas owed you except for da nigga from West Philly. He been duckin me but when I catch him I'ma fuck him up."

"What he owe?"

"Da whole one-twenty."

"He ain't pay none of it?"

"Nope."

"Want me to talk to him?" I ask.

"Na you ain't gotta talk to him. Talkin is over. He been playin games wit me for two months now. I'm done playin."

"Do what you think is best. How da block runnin?"

"I got it unda control. I gave Lisette ya cut da otha day."

"She told me. What bout Tone and Spud's cut?" "I gave Tone's cut to Rosie and I called Becca but she ain't answer her phone. I got da money. I'm just waitin for her to come and get it."

"Keep callin till you get in touch wit her."

"Maybe when I leave here I'll stop past her crib and see what's up."

"Do dat and when you see her make sure you tell her dat when she know it's time to collect dat she be available cause if something happen to you before she collect den it's her loss."

"What about you yo, you need anything?"

"I'm cool."

"I wish it was something I could do beijo."

"I know but it ain't. All you can do now is hold me down from da outside. You my lifeline. When it come to street shit you da only one I got left."

"I know. You know you ain't gotta worry bout shit while

I'm on da streets. I'ma always take care of you," Bebe told me and I could tell he was sincere.

"I know you is." I said touching fists with my young bul who affectionately called me his stepfather.

* * * * *

AUGUST 1995

I may have thought I was getting money before but I was fooling myself. The money that I made case working was nothing compared to the money that me, Tone and Mama were pulling in now that we were owners of the corner. I was making so much money that I didn't know what to do with it. I was young and on the fast track to being rich. The one thing I wasn't was stupid so I made sure that my family was well taken care of.

The first thing I did when I started to see good money was to find a place for me and Lisette to live. We were going to get an apartment but then she found out that she was pregnant again and we knew that we needed something bigger. Last month Lisette went through a few days where she wasn't feeling well so she went to the doctor. It was then that she found out that she was four weeks pregnant.

Her mom and dad helped us get a nice three bedroom house in the Northeast, far away from the ghetto and the business that I did. The next thing I did with some of my money was rent me an apartment that no one but me knew about. In this apartment I installed a safe where I could keep my money. This would be my emergency money. Hopefully, I would conduct business well enough that I would never have to tell anybody about it.

Rosie giving us the corner was definitely the best thing that ever happened to us and day by day it got better. So far our only problem had been with Joel but ever since that night everything had been calm. Joel was the only one to live and we hadn't heard from him or seen him since then. We weren't worried one way or the other.

The first few days after the shootout we were a little worried but then word got back to us that the detectives wanted to talk to us but only for questioning. We were the main suspects but they didn't have enough to charge us with the murders. When we heard this we all contacted lawyers who in turn urged us to turn ourselves in for questioning which we did reluctantly.

We were interrogated for hours but none of us gave them anything and eventually they gave up and let us go. When we were all released we talked about what they had asked each of us and the questions were basically the same. One thing we all had to admit was that the detectives knew exactly what had happened which meant that there had been people who told. None of that mattered to us because we also knew that when they didn't charge us it meant that while people had told, they had done it without making official statements. Our mark had been made. People in the hood knew that to tell on us meant death. Tone had made that point loud and clear when he had killed the witness on my other case.

With the homicide off of our backs we went to work on our block. We knew that the detectives were still working the case trying to get enough evidence to lock us up but we didn't care. We had one goal. Get money and we set about doing that with a fury.

The first thing we did was to brand our product. The name that we came up with was Punisher. We called it that because that's what it did to our friends. It punished them. Our bags were stamped with the emblem from the Punisher comics and fiends came from far and wide for our dope.

The next thing we did was to solidify our position. Mama played a big part in this because while me and Tone knew a lot of people, Mama knew who they really were. When it came time for us to hire some kind of security for the corner, Mama was able to point us in the right direction. She knew whether an individual was a ryda or not. She knew who wouldn't hesitate to bust their gun and she knew who was really a killer as opposed to a nigga just being a pussy with a gun. Mama handled most of this phase and she did a great job because all of the dudes she hired would work for us until we came to jail.

Once we established everything we simply sat back and watched the money roll in. It was August and we had owned the corner for six months now and we had made our mark among the elite of Da Bad Landz. It wasn't like before where certain people knew who I was or only certain people spoke to me. Now everyone knew who I was and everyone spoke. Not only was I known but I was treated like an equal. The biggest example I had of this was on a hot day in August when the biggest and at the time most feared nigga in our hood sat and talked with me.

It was late afternoon and I was sitting on my usual perch when I saw Teddy pull up and get out of his car. He walked over to his worker Pudge who was still hustling on our corner. Teddy talked to him for about ten minutes then as he was heading back to his car he spotted me and walked over. While he walked in my direction, I observed how many people spoke to him and the manner in which they spoke to him. I had never, since I had been in this neighborhood seen a black guy get so much respect. It didn't matter who he came across, whether it be a boss or a fiend, the level of respect or fear depending on how you looked at it was the same.

"What's up Pooh?" Teddy asked as he approached and shook my hand.

"I'm chilhn. What's up wit you?"

"Just doin da same thing you doin, watchin over my money. I been hearin good things bout what y'all doin out here."

"We tryin."

"Y'all ain't tryin playa y'all doin it. Yo . . ."

"Pooh let me ask you something," one of my workers said interrupting Teddy who turned to the worker and looked at him like he was crazy.

"Yo, what's ya fuckin problem? Don't you see two bosses talkin? Have some fuckin respect," Teddy said chastising the worker who immediately put his head down and walked away.

"Why you bark on him like dat?" I asked.

"So he know his place," he told me and I didn't understand what he was talking about. I think he could sense this and began to break it down to me.

"Pooh you and ya peoples bosses now and y'all bosses of a major corner. You gotta separate yaself from da workers. Dey gotta know dey place. It's about respect da respect dat dey pose to show you. When dey see you talkin dey pose to wait to be addressed before dey speak. If dat was one of my workers dey would have stood there for a hour before dey would have interrupted me."

"I feel what you sayin but I just be tryin to treat everybody equal."

"I respect dat and I don't wanna try to tell you how to run ya business but I dig you, so I don't wanna see you make no dumb mistakes either."

"I feel you and I appreciate it."

"Let me ask you dis. How long you had da block?"

"Six months."

"If you had to could you put ya hands on a hundred grand of ya own money?"

"Yeah," I said confidently and felt good saying it.

"Den deez niggas niggas ain't ya equals. Deez niggas ain't nothin but workers. Treat em as such. If one of ya workers is more den a worker to you den find him another position but everybody else you treat accordingly. Dis is a business and da bottom line is dat most of da niggas workin for you don't really give a fuck about you. Dey only act like dey do because you feedin em. If dat stop dey true colors will show, believe me."

"I ain't think about it like dat."

"Don't worry neither did I until someone who knew da game schooled me. Oh and another thing. Don't never expose to nobody how much money you can put ya hands on. Niggas will try anything for a little bit of paper."

"I only said something cause it was you."

"I know but remember dat you don't know me dat well and I might be a snake. You never know who you dealin wit in deez streets so it's always best to keep niggas at arms reach so you can keep an eye on em. I gotta get outta here and take care of some business but I get back wit you," Teddy said and shook my hand. He turned to walk away then turned back to me.

"I heard about da work y'all been puttin in out here and dats good. Fear is always da best repellent when you fuckin wit da niggas dat we fuck wit on a daily basis. Respect is good when making friends but when it comes to making money fear is a hustla's best utensil. A wise old head told me dat back in da day and it's da truest shit I eva heard. Just do ya thing Pooh and you'll be aiight. Get wit me if you need anything. You know where to find me." Teddy walked to his car and got in then pulled off.

When he was gone I digested everything he said and all of it made a whole lot of sense. Right then and there I started mentally implementing into my style the things that Teddy had told me. I had plans on changing my style so that I could achieve the longevity I had seen some other hustlas have.

From that day on I would treat my workers as exactly that. I wouldn't be merciless when dealing with them. If they needed my assistance I would help them but they would definitely know where our relationship stood. I was their boss and they were my workers. The only one who wouldn't be treated like that would be Bebe who from that day on would be my protege.

I would take him under my wing and begin molding him

to take my place if anything should ever happen to me. Over the next few weeks I would test him numerous times and he would always pass all them. Every time he passed a test the next one got a little harder. But no matter how hard it got he always prevailed. I knew that I had made the right choice.

Chapter 15

MAY 2001

C.F.C.F UNIT D2-1

"A hoendo esta mi pana."

I am in my cell when I hear this but I instantly know who it is. I step out my cell and look up to the desk where Spud and Tone are both standing with their belongings. I jog to them and one by one I hug both of my brothers. Mi-Mi and Daniels looked at us for a minute before interrupting us and telling Spud and Tone what cell they were in. They were both going in the cell next to me. There had been two other dudes in there but they were now on another block so that room could be made for my niggas.

I walk them to their cell and we all enter. While they begin to clean up and set their stuff up I tell them what's going on on the block specifically about Mi-Mi and who she is to me. It takes them an hour to get the cell in order and once they are done we go out onto the block and sit at one of the tables. Stiz sees us and walks over to where we are sitting. Instantly Spud and Tone go silent.

"Pooh what's up?"

"Ain't shit. Stiz deez my brothers Spud and Tone. Dis Stiz y'all," I say making introductions.

They all shake hands then Stiz attempts to sit down but Tone stops him.

"We talkin right now homie."

"Oh my bad," Stiz apologizes.

"It's cool," Tone says as he walks away.

"Who's dat?"

"He aiight. I know him from back in da day," I say and Tone simply nods his head.

I see Spuds eyes lift and I follow them until I see what he is focusing on. It's Mi-Mi and both Tone and Spud have their eyes glued to her as does every other nigga in the dayroom.

"Hello," she says as she gets to the table.

"What's up?" I ask.

"Nothin. You goin introduce me or what?"

"Tone, Spud dis is Mi-Mi. Deez is my brothers Spud and Tone. She da one dat got y'all moved on da block."

"Gracia mami," Spud says.

"What he say?"

"He said thank you," I tell her.

"Esta mami esta bueno," Tone says then laughs.

"And what he say."

"He said you a bad bitch," I say while laughing and she laughs too.

"Thank you," she tells Tone then turns to me. "I'll see you later, right?" she asks me.

"Ain't no doubt," I respond and she walks off.

I tell them about me and her meeting in the education building and they both laugh.

"Dis pretty muthafucka think he a pimp," Spud says while nudging Tone.

"Nigga you know I'ma pimp. You know bitches love me."

"What's up wit Ronnie?" Tone asks me.

"She cool. She comin to see me dis week."

"Yo remember when she pissed on herself?"

Tone asked with a smile that after realizing what he had said quickly faded.

I remembered this vividly and obviously so did Tone because when I look at him I can see the sorrow in his eyes. I know that I have the same look in my eyes. The day in question was funny at first then it quickly turned tragic for us.

* * * * *

SEPTEMBER 1995

As long as I live I'll never forget the day September 4th, 1995. The day started out great but it wouldn't end that way. It was about four o'clock in the afternoon. Me, Tone, Mama, Bebe and Ronnie were sitting on a set of steps laughing and joking. Me and Ronnie looked like a couple but I wasn't worried about getting caught because

Lisette and her family had gone to Puerto Rico for a week. They had been gone for three days already and Ronnie had been with me for those three days. She still didn't mind me having a girl that I lived with and if she didn't mind then I definitely didn't mind having her around.

Bebe who now lived with me and Lisette was taking to the role of my protege. He had matured so much from when I first hired him that Tone now saw what I saw in him. Bebe had been living with me and Lisette for a month. He was so glad to be in a home where the people there cared about him that he had started calling Lisette mom. This day he was doing exactly what everyone else was doing having a good time with each other.

At one point while we were sitting there Mama and Tone left to go get some drinks. When they returned they had three bottles of Alize. Ronnie who was sort of new to all the shit we were into was scared to drink at first but we finally broke her. The next thing you know she was drinking cup after cup of the liquor like it was water. I tried to tell her to slow down but she was drunk and having too much fun to stop. We all got tipsy but Ronnie got fucked up to the point where she couldn't stand. Then it happened.

I don't know where he got them from but Tone always seemed to have a joke to tell and today was no different. He began to tell the joke and when he was done everyone laughed until we were in tears. When the commotion finally calmed down Ronnie grabbed my hand and said that she needed my help and 1 asked her what she needed. She didn't say anything but she did start laughing. Then through her laughter she managed to tell me that she had pissed on herself.

As soon as she said it everyone looked down and realized that she wasn't lying. There was a stream of piss running over the concrete and everyone started laughing again. Ronnie who didn't seem the least bit embarrassed laughed right along with us until I helped her up and led her to Rosie's house. At Rosie's I helped her into the shower then asked Rosie for some clothes. Rosie gave me some fresh panties for her then gave me a t-shirt and a pair of jeans for her to put on.

I was helping Ronnie out of the shower when I heard the sound of gunfire and lots of it. I quickly led Ronnie to Rosie's room and laid her down on the bed. I rushed down the steps of the house and to the front door snatching it open. When I stuck my head out the door I saw Tone standing behind a car exchanging shots with two niggas. I realized that one of them was Joel, our former case worker.

I snatched my gun off my waist and ran full speed down the block. As soon as I was close enough I started shooting. I only got off about four shots before Joel and whoever was with him got back into their car and peeled off. Tone ran to the corner and looked as if he was going to chase the car but didn't. Instead he turned and walked back to where I was standing.

"What da fuck happened?" I asked him.

"I don't know. Dem niggas just pulled up and started shootin."

"You seen who it was right?"

"Yeah, it was Joel. I'ma kill dat pussy."

I could hear the sirens in the distance and looked around

for Bebe who was approaching. I gave him my gun. Tone did the same then I told him to take them to Rosie's house. Just as he was heading up the street I realized something and swung my head from side to side, not finding who I was looking for.

"Yo, where da fuck is Mama?" I asked.

"I don't know. She went that way when the shooting started," Tone said pointing in the direction of Rosie's house.

"She ain't have her gun on her?" I asked.

"Na, she left it at the crib."

I called out her name but received no response so I called out again netting the same results. I walked in the direction that Tone had said she went and after taking four steps I spotted a familiar pair of white and pink Nikes sticking out from in between two cars. I quickened my pace and when I got to the pair of sneakers my heart sank into my stomach and my knees went weak.

I used one of the cars for support as I looked at Mama laying in between the two cars bleeding from two gunshots to her back. The blood was pouring out of her wounds and it took all the strength I had to summon Tone to where I was. Tone arrived three seconds after I called him. He immediately kneeled down in between the cars and rolled her over onto her side. Her eyes were closed and a trickle of blood ran out of the corner of her mouth. Tone yelled for someone to call for an ambulance but we both knew that it was useless. She wasn't breathing and she just looked like she had no shot of making it. I knelt down with Tone and he did something that shocked me. He grabbed my hand then grabbed Mama's hand and began to pray.

A crowd began to form around us but Tone could have cared less. He prayed and asked God to accept our sister into heaven. When he was done we both had tears in our eyes. We didn't care about anybody seeing the tears. This was our sister and she deserved to be cried over. When Tone finished praying we both kissed Mama on her forehead then stood to our feet. As we were standing the cops were walking towards us so we went through the bullshit questions that they asked us. When they were done with us we both headed to Rosie's with Mama's blood all over our clothes.

"Shut da block down," Tone told me.

"For what?"

"We don't hustle on dis day no more out of respect for Mama."

"What about Joel?"

"What about him?" Tone asked.

"When we goin go get dat nigga?"

"How fast can you grab ya gun?" Tone asked as we entered

the house.

* * * * *

We rode around for two hours looking for Joel but couldn't find him. We had circled 5th and Westmoreland numerous times but he was nowhere to be found. We had just turned onto 5th and Ontario when a car sped past us and cut us off. Not knowing what was going on, me and Tone both pulled our guns off of our waist and began to open our doors. To our surprise it was Teddy that had cut us off. He gave us a signal to stay in the car but Tone got out anyway so I followed his lead. Later he would tell me that at that point he didn't know what vibe Teddy was on and didn't want to take any chances.

"What da fuck is y'all doin? Put y'all guns away," Teddy told us then called out to Boo who emerged from the passenger's seat.

"Drive da car to Hancock. We'll follow you," Teddy told him and Boo got into the driver's seat.

"Let me ride wit y'all," Teddy said and got into the back seat. We got in the front seat and Teddy leaned forward.

"Why y'all out here trippin?" he asked.

"We ain't trippin. We lookin for da nigga dat killed our sister," Tone said.

"I respect dat but y'all still trippin."

"How?" Tone asked.

"Dis ain't Hancock and Cambria where y'all can just kill some niggas and get away wit it. Deez niggas goin tell on y'all."

"Yo. I don't give a fuck bout none of dat. Da nigga killed Mama and he gotta die."

"I ain't sayin you wrong for wantin revenge. I'm just sayin dat you doin it wrong."

"What we pose to do den?" I ask speaking for the first time.

"Y'all gotta think. Y'all big time now which mean y'all gotta do everything smarter den before. I ain't sayin don't kill da nigga cause da nigga deserve to die. I'm just sayin be smart about killin him."

"So what you think we should do?" Tone asked as he turned onto Hancock Street.

"Just chill for a couple hours and let me see if I can find where da nigga at for y'all. Dat'll make it a little easier for y'all."

"Why you helping us?" Tone questioned.

"Cause ya old head is my family and dat makes y'all my family. I dig y'all whole style and I don't want to see y'all run cut short by y'all makin a dumb mistake," Teddy said as we all got out of the car.

"How long we goin have to chill?" I asked Teddy.

"At least until tomorrow. Let da shit die down and let me see what I can do. If I can't find da nigga den tomorrow y'all do what y'all gotta do."

"Aiight we'll chill for da night," Tone said. Teddy nodded his head then shook our hands.

He was on his way to the car that Boo was sitting in when I called out to him. He turned to face me and asked me what was up.

"If you find him, don't kill him."

"I wouldn't do no shit like dat. Dat's for y'all to handle," he said then walked to his car.

Me and Tone walked to Rosie's both fuming over what had happened and both feeling impatient about waiting to extract revenge. We wanted to still be out there looking for Joel but we had agreed to wait and let Teddy see what he could do so that's what we were going to do. The result would definitely end up being worth the wait.

* * * * *

It was three in the morning. Me and Tone were drunk, high and grieving. I had never felt so much pain in my entire life. Seeing Mama like that earlier had initially hurt me but once we chilled out and had more time to think about it, it tore me apart. Mama wasn't like a sister to me. She was my sister and now she was gone. I felt the tears welling up again and wiped my eyes. I looked at Tone who also had tears in his eyes and he said nothing. He took a puff of the wet blunt that he was smoking and fondled the gun that he had in his lap. A knock on the door startled both of us. Tone jumped up with his gun ready and went to the door. He aimed the gun at the door then asked who it was. He lowered the gun once he heard that it was Teddy.

"Take a ride wit me," Teddy said not entering the house when Tone opened the door.

"Where?" Tone asked.

"Don't ask no questions just ride," Teddy said then walked down the street.

Tone didn't say anything. He just put his gun on his waist and followed. I too put my gun on my waist and followed Tone down the street. We got into the back of a car that Teddy was driving with Boo riding shotgun. There were no words spoken as we drove the short distance to 7th and Indiana. We all got out of the car and even though it was three in the morning Teddy's corner was still jumping.

Teddy led us to a house in the middle of 7th Street. He opened the door and motioned for us to enter. Tone hesitated but Teddy reassured him that everything was cool. Tone pulled his gun off of his waist. I followed suit and Teddy laughed as we entered. When we were all inside he informed us that if he wanted to harm us that he would have done it.

He walked ahead of us and headed down the basement steps. When we reached the basement we could hear a noise like someone was whimpering but the lights were out so we could see nothing. A few seconds later Teddy pulled a string hanging from the ceiling illuminating the basement with a single bulb. Tied to a chair in the middle of the floor was Joel and some other nigga.

"Dis is how I managed to stay on da streets dis long. I learned how to do shit smarter. Dis right here is da best lesson I could eva give y'all. Ain't nothing wrong with killing. It makes da life we live go round and most niggas dat we kill deserve to die. You just gotta make sure you smart about it."

"Who da otha nigga?" I asked him.

"Da otha shooter."

"How you find dem?" Tone questioned.

"It ain't nothin in dis hood dat I can't do and if y'all play y'all cards right y'all goin be da same way."

"Thanx."

"Don't thank me, just take care of y'all business," Teddy said as he walked past us and up the steps leaving us alone with

Joel and his homie.

I raised my gun to shoot Joel but Tone stopped me, he bowed his head and said another silent prayer.

"What you pray for dis time?" I asked him.

"I asked God to tell Mama dat we got dem niggas for her."

"You can't ask God to tell Mama dat we killed some niggas for her."

"I just did. You ready?" Tone asked motioning to the two captives.

"Yeah, I'm ready."

We both raised our guns and before we shot, Tone reminded me to save some shells for Joel's homie. I nodded my head and without further hesitation we both began firing. I fired eight times then stopped while Tone kept firing until his gun was empty. I quickly stepped over to our other victim and put the rest of the bullets in my gun into his head. Mama had been avenged properly and contrary to popular belief it did make me feel better.

* * * *

JUNE 2001

C.F.C.F UNIT D2-1

"So what y'all wanna do?"

"I don't care," Spud answers.

"Me either," Tone says.

"I mean it don't make no sense for us to be sittin in dis county all dis time when we could be upstate wit TV's and shit."

"You talked to ya lawyer?" Tone asks me.

"He comin today."

"Do it. I don't care. I'll tell my lawyer da same thing when I call him," Tone tells me.

"I'ma do whateva y'all do," Spud says.

"Aught I'ma tell him to get us in court soon so we can get da fuck out of dis county."

"What y'all think we goin get?" Spud questions. "It depends," Tone replies.

"Depends on what?"

"What kind of jury we get and how good da lawyers fight."

Tone said this last statement then picks up his newspaper. Out of the three of us he is the only one of us who reads the paper everyday. In fact, me and Spud rarely ever read it. We really have no interest in what is going on if it doesn't concern us. Me and Spud continue to talk while Tone reads then he startles us.

"Oh shit," Tone exclaims.

"What?" I ask.

"Yo, what's ya homie name?"

"What homie?"

"Da one on da block dat be wit us?"

"Stiz. Why?"

"Ain't his real name Steven Rice?"

"Yeah, how you know dat?"

"I saw his armband one day."

"Why you askin questions bout him?" I ask, Tone wondering what is going on.

"He a rat," Tone says.

"What?"

"He at court today right?"

"Yeah, he said da judge was going to rule on one of his motions."

"Dats bullshit. Dat nigga at court testifying on somebody look," Tone tells me and holds up the article he is reading.

I begin to read the article and I can't believe what I am reading. The article talks about Stiz testifying on a Federal Indictment in Delaware County. It tells how Stiz who was once under investigation along with the other fifteen niggas who are now indicted, escaped prosecution by agreeing to testify for the prosecutor. The article doesn't say what he actually testified to but it does say that today when he takes the stand that it will seal the fate of all of the defendants.

I finish reading the article then give it another once over and hand it back to Tone who reads it again then laughs. It takes a few seconds for what I just read to register but when it does I become infuriated. I'm mad because this nigga has been chilling with me everyday like he a standup dude and the whole time he's a rat. Spud looks in my face and as if he's reading my mind he verbalizes exactly what I am thinking.

"You wanna fuck him up?"

"Yeah, I wanna fuck dat nigga up," I respond.

"Say no more," Tone chimes in.

* * * * *

"Yo, Stiz let's go in ya cell and blow dis weed," I say as I walk up on him.

"Come on."

"My brothers comin wit us."

"Dats cool. Dey ya peoples."

"Aught let's go," I tell him and he leads the way to his cell.

Stiz had been back from court since before count but I decided to wait until the jail opened before punishing him. We get to his cell and he tells his celly to step out for a while which he does. Two minutes after his celly leaves Tone and Spud appear and I roll a stick of weed. I hand the stick to Stiz who stands on a chair in front of the vent. I give him the lighter. He lights the weed and takes two puffs. While he's holding the smoke in from the second puff I snatch the chair from under his feet. He falls hard to the cell floor and looks up at me trying to figure out what is going on.

"You was just goin chill wit me knowing you was a rat, huh?"

"What you talkin bout Pooh?"

"Dis what da fuck I'm talkin bout," I say and pull the article out of my pocket throwing it at him.

He looks at it then back up at me. "It ain't what it look like Pooh."

"It look like you a fuckin rat."

"Da prosecutors made me tell."

"Wrong answer," I say and kick him in his face. I

punch and kick him for about two minutes then I let Tone and Spud go at him for a few minutes. Once Stiz stops moving I stop them from hitting him for fear that he might die. He lays there motionless so I grab a cup and throw two cups of cold toilet water on his face. He finally comes to. He is dazed but alert.

"Clean yaself da fuck up den take p.c. pussy and keep ya fuckin mouth shut bout how you got fucked up," I tell him. Then we step over him and out of the cell.

As we exit the cell Mi-Mi looks up at us then averts her attention to some nigga who is asking her a question. I walk to the desk and she gets rid of the nigga. I tell her what happened and what Stiz is going to do. I also tell her that if he tries to tell on us that she has to say that he is lying. She tells me not to worry about anything and I nod my head. I go to my cell and tell Tone and Spud what she said, then we smoke some weed while laughing about how bad we fucked Stiz up.

Chapter 16

DECEMBER 1995

Christmas was a week away and from the looks of my house you could tell. There were Christmas lights everywhere. Our tree was huge and there were loads of presents stacked under it. Lisette who was big on holidays was having a little get together for our family and friends and the house was packed. In attendance was all of Lisette's family. Her mom and dad, her brothers and sisters and all of their kids were present. Rosie and Tone were there as was Bebe who really didn't count though because he lived there.

Rebecca Spud's baby mom was there along with their son. Becca's sister Jennifer was there and flirting with me heavily. Even two of my aunts from Jose's side of the family showed up. These were the only two people on that side of the family who didn't fault me for what had happened to him. They were into the streets and knew what had went down.

All around me my family and friends were having a great time but I just could not get into the spirit and I knew exactly why. Every time I looked around the room at all of the smiling faces there was always one missing. I looked at the picture hanging on my living room wall and there was the missing smiling face. Just looking at the picture cheered me up a little but also reminded me how much I missed Mama.

When she first died the pain was bad but I had no idea that it would still hurt this bad three months later. The pain that I was still feeling made me realize how much of an impact Mama had on my growth and how much I loved her. I now spoke Spanish fluently because of her and because of her I also had an angel dust habit. For the longest time I had only trusted four people in the entire world. Now there were only three. Two of them were in my living room and the third was in jail but would hopefully be home this upcoming summer.

Speaking of Spud he called earlier to talk to everyone and wish them happy holidays. He is now closer to the city being as though he got kicked out of the place the courts had sent him to. The reason they kicked him out was because he had assaulted a staff member. He had been in New Castle but now he was in Cornwall Heights.

Today was actually the first time that I had spoken to Spud in about six or seven months but trust me it was through no fault of my own. Spud didn't call anyone regularly except Becca and that was only to check on his son. He said that while he was in jail he didn't focus on the streets so that his time would go by quicker. I let him do his bid the way he wanted to. Every two or three weeks I would send him a stack of about fifty pictures of friends, family and random bitches. Chicks on the streets, chicks either me or Tone had been fucking with in their panties and Spud's all-time favorite strippers. He loved pictures of strippers in their thongs so with every stack of flicks I made sure that I sent at least fifteen shots of strippers.

"What's wrong?" Rosie said coming over to sit next to me.

"I'm aiight."

"No you not."

"It's just dat I wish Mama was here wit us."

"Me too."

"Pooh I ain't know Lisette could cook like dat." Tone said.

Tone loved to eat and he loved anyone who could cook good food. He sat next to Rosie and rubbed his stomach then let out a loud burp.

"Excuse me," he said.

I looked at Tone and Rosie then at all the other people who were there. It was then that I realized that while I was saddened by Mama's death there was still a lot that I had to be happy about. I stroked the portrait of Mama that me and Tone had tattooed on our arms and smiled. The entire tattoo included not only Mama's face but her whole upper body. Above her head was a halo and on her back was a set of angels wings. Her name, date of birth and the day she died was under the portrait. All of this ran from where my shoulder began down to my elbow.

Just running my fingers across it made me feel better. It was like I could feel Mama's presence and the feeling was great. I cheered up instantly and got into the groove of celebrating the holidays with my family. I ate, drank and enjoyed the company of the people that I knew loved me. We partied into the night until everyone finally got tired and began to disperse. Becca who I had picked up waited patiently until I finished arguing with Lisette's father over who was better, the Eagles or the Giants so I could take her home. I told Lisette what I was doing then headed out the house carrying Lil Alex, Spud's son.

Becca sat in the passengers seat and I handed her Lil Alex while Jennifer climbed into the back seat. Everyone was silent so the ride to their house was quiet. When we got there I helped Becca in the house and promised to bring the presents that we had forgotten at my house in the next few days. I kissed Alex on his forehead then headed back out to my car where Jennifer was waiting on me.

Jennifer who was now 19 had blossomed into a thing of beauty. I mean she was pretty back in the day when I first met her but now she was a sight to behold. Her beauty had enhanced her status with a lot of the hustlas in my hood and the word about her that I got was that she was now a super whore. I would see her from time to time on the block or somewhere in the vicinity. Every time she was with a different dude so I knew what was on her mind when I came out of the house and she was leaning on my car.

"You leavin Pooh?"

"Yeah I'm tired. I gotta go get some rest."

"Why don't you chill wit me for a while?"

"Why would I do dat?" I asked as I got to where she was standing and posted up in front of her.

"I ain't see you for a while."

"You see me all da time. You just spent da whole night at my house. Why you ain't try to chill wit me den?"

"Too many people was there."

"Na, you mean my girl was there."

"Whateva. Same thing."

"What you want yo cause I gotta go."

"I just told you what I want. I wanna chill wit you."

"Back when we use to fuck wit each otha and I went broke,

you ain't wanna chill wit me den," I said and tried to walk past her but she stopped me by reaching out and grabbing my dick.

"Let me show you how sorry I am for being a stupid ass," she said then put her hand down the front of my pants.

"What you doin yo?"

"I'm tryin to apologize."

I looked back at her house making sure that no one was paying attention to what was going on. I turned back to her and by then my dick was hard and she was massaging it with her hand.

"Dig dis if you open ya mouth about what happens between us we gain have a problem."

"What kind of problem?" she asked with a smile on her face.

"A big one."

"You don't have to threaten me Pooh."

"I ain't threatenin you. I'm makin you a promise."

"Oh what Pooh. You goin beat me up?" she asked as if I was playing.

"If you put my business in the streets and it get back to Lisette and ruin my relationship, fuck no I ain't goin beat you up I'ma murda you," I said and looked her dead in her eye so if she was smart she would be able to tell that I was serious.

She returned the look that I gave her and continued to play with my dick letting me know that she still wanted to get down so I told her to get into the front seat of my car and she did. I drove around the corner from her house to a dark side street and parked. I pulled my dick out of my jeans, then grabbed the back of her head guiding her mouth to where I wanted it to be.

Back when we used to fuck with each other she had never sucked my dick so this was a first, a wonderful first. Jennifer was like a pro with my dick in her mouth. So much of a pro that after only a few minutes of her sucking I found myself about to cum. I grabbed the back of her neck and forced her head down more and she obliged me with no resisting or hesitation. She sucked with fury and before I knew it I was shooting my cum all over the back of her throat. I held her in place until I was finished cumming then let her up. She wiped the corners of her mouth with her fingers then began to undo her pants.

"What you doin?" I questioned.

"I want you to fuck me."

"I ain't got no condom."

"I got one," she told me and held up the Trojan in her hand.

I thought for a second and when I looked back at her she already had her pants and panties off. Her pussy was covered with a bush of black hair that she was stroking with her fingers. I watched as she stopped stroking and placed two of her fingers inside of her pussy and fingered herself. She did this for about a minute then pulled the fingers out and sucked the juices off of them. That was it. My dick was hard as a brick and I had to something about it.

I undid the button and zipper on my jeans and began taking them off because there was no way I was going to run the risk of her juices staining the black jeans that I had on. Once I had them off I told her to climb into the back seat and she did. I climbed back there with her and even though it was cold out I hit the button to lower one of the rear windows. I made her lean her arms on the door frame and stick her head out the window while she was on her knees.

I quickly slid the condom on, then placed two of my fingers in her pussy to make sure that it was wet. It was. I removed my fingers and slid my dick inside of her. Her walls enveloped me as I penetrated her all the way to my base. Her head was out the window but I could still hear her moan.

I began to pump fast and hard causing her to moan loudly, so loud in fact that I thought she was going to wake a few of the residents on the block. I wouldn't have cared if they did wake up or if they came out of their houses and watched. Jennifer had some good pussy and I intended to fuck the shit out of her until I came.

I slammed away at her pussy with all of my might and she took it like the pro I had heard she was. Her ass cheeks rippled every time my pelvis met them and during these meetings was when she moaned the loudest. Eventually these moans turned into urges from her for me to fuck her harder. Finally she moaned that she was about to cum. I picked my pace up and she began to grind her ass back into me. Two minutes into this she shuddered and moaned that she came. I fucked her for about a minute more before I too came then slid out of her.

I sat in the car seat and she pulled herself back into the car and sat also. My dick was going soft but the condom was still on it so I told her to get rid of it. To my surprise she bent over and removed the condom with her teeth. I was so in awe of what she was doing that it wasn't until she had spit the condom out the window that I realized my cum had spilled on me. I was getting ready to curse her out when she bent again and began to lick all of the spilled cum off of me.

"You wanna go again?" she asked me.

"You trippin. I just busted twice. It's ova for me."

"I bet you I can make you cum again."

"Cum, you crazy. I ain't even goin get hard again."

"Wanna bet?" she said and took my soft dick into her mouth.

She licked and sucked my dick then went to my balls and did the same thing. She muttered all types of freaky shit to me and before I knew it I was getting hard again. Once I was fully hard again she sat up and smiled at me while retrieving another condom. She opened it and rolled it down my dick. I told her that it was going to be forever before I came but she promised me that it wouldn't be.

Once she had the condom on me she made me slide to the middle of the seat then she straddled me. She eased herself down and began to ride me. She closed her eyes and began to make some of the sexiest fuck faces I had ever seen. She rode up and down and just like I figured it was going to be a long time before I nutted. She rode me for about ten minutes with her eyes close. It felt great but I was not even close to cumming. Finally she re-opened her eyes and asked me if I was ready. I looked at her like she was crazy because I had been ready and we had been fucking for ten minutes already.

Without waiting for my answer she raised up and my dick came out of her. She grabbed it with her hand, steadied it then began to lower herself again. I noticed her positioning herself differently as she began her descent. The minute I penetrated her I knew it wasn't her pussy. It was too tight and too warm. She moaned loudly as she sat all the way down and took my whole dick into her ass.

She began to go up and down slowly making me fell sensations that I had never felt before. This was my first time fucking a girl in her ass. Slowly but surely she picked her pace up and contrary to what I believed a few minutes of this and I felt myself ready to cum. She continued with her grinding and I grabbed hold of her hips tightly. I think she could sense that I was about to cum because she grinded harder until I released my nut with a loud moan.

I pulled her to me and rested my head on her chest while she gyrated her ass, sucking all of my cum out of me. When I finished I let her waist go and she got up off of my dick. She took the condom off of me and threw it out of the window just like she had done with the other one. Just like before, she licked and sucked the cum off of me then she climbed back over into the front seat to get dressed. I got out of the car and grabbed my pants putting them on. Then I got back into the drivers seat and started the car. I drove back around the corner to her house. Before getting out she looked at me.

"When we gonna do dis again?" she asked me.

"As long as you keep it to yaself we can do dis shit all da time."

"Alright I'll see you later," she said then got out.

As soon as she was out I pulled off but instead of heading home I headed to the block. I was going to go to Rosie's because there was no way I could go home smelling like this.

* * * * *

The two weeks following my episode with Jennifer was crazy. At least ten days out of that fourteen we got together so she could fuck or suck me. This day I was sitting in my car on the block smoking weed with Bebe while my beeper went off continuously. Every time it went off it was Jennifer. She had been paging me all day and I had been ducking her. Truth be told she was wearing me out, the sex was out of this world but she was killing me. I would fuck her for two or three hours then I would have to go home and fuck Lisette for at least an hour. Not to mention the other bitches I might encounter on any given day. All of this combined was killing me.

I passed the blunt to Bebe and once again checked my beeper, I laughed when I saw Jennifer's phone number. I cleared the number from my memory but a few minutes later I was doing the same thing again.

"Who keep beepin you yo?" Bebe asked me.

"Some horny bitch."

"Why you don't call her back?"

"Cause I don't feel like fuckin."

"Why?"

"Cause I'm tired. Why you wanna fuck her?"

Bebe passed me the blunt back and turned his head to his window without answering my question.

"Yo, you can answer. I ain't goin get mad if you say yeah."

"I'm cool," he responded with his head still turned to the window.

"What's up wit you yo? You aiight?" I asked.

"Yeah I'm cool."

I puffed the blunt a few times then handed it back to Bebe who puffed it. He exhaled the smoke and looked at me for a minute.

"Yo, if I tell you somethin you ain't goin tell nobody else right?" he asked me.

"Anything you eva say to me goin stay between you and me unless you say it's okay to say somethin to someone. Dats how it is between homies."

"I'm a virgin. Dats why I told you I ain't wanna fuck her."

"You a virgin." I said and chuckled.

He gave me the blunt back and turned his head to the window again. I knew that my chuckling had hurt his feelings and I felt bad because I ain't want him to think that I was making fun of him.

"Yo, I ain't mean to laugh at you."

"It's cool," he said still looking out the window.

"You want some pussy?" I asked him.

"Don't no bitches wanna give me no pussy."

"You trippin yo. You could get all da bitches you want if you try."

"How?"

"Let's do dis. Let's get you some pussy first, den we'll work on how you goin get bitches." I said starting the car and pulling off.

* * * * *

JULY 2001

C.F.C.F UNIT D2-1

I did get Bebe his first piece of pussy that day. When we pulled off I drove to Jennifer's house. I explained to her about my young bul and told her that she was going to bless him the way that she always blessed me and she did. Later that night when I seen Bebe again he had a huge kool-aid smile on his face. This alone let me know that Jennifer had treated him right.

I fucked with Jennifer for a couple months after that, then I left her alone. I started getting reports of her helping some black dude set niggas up to get robbed. When I asked her about it she told me that it was true but swore that she had never even considered doing something like that to me.

It didn't matter to me whether she considered it or not I wasn't willing to take that risk. After I stopped fucking with her the stories got crazier. There were even two stories floating that ended with there being a bounty on Jennifer's head. By then she wasn't living with Becca anymore, which was a good thing. If something was to happen to Becca or Lil Alex because someone was looking for Jennifer there would be hell to pay. Not only would whoever was responsible die but so would Jennifer.

From what I hear Jennifer and whoever this black guy is made a killing off of their robberies. Their M.O was simple. Jennifer and her pretty ass would seduce their victim then fuck him and suck him till he was wide open. She would have him so open that he would never see it coming but would remember it forever. They plied their trade mainly in neighborhoods where dudes weren't use to Puerto Rican girls. They had garnered a few victims from Da Bad Landz and Hunting Park which were predominately Puerto Rican neighborhoods but their best work was done in all black neighborhoods. All she ever did was change her name and hair color.

I gave you Jennifer's back story so you could fully understand what type of chick she was. She had been setting niggas up for close to six years now and if the rumors that I heard were even close to true then she was sitting on some nice money. She was definitely going to need that money to pay for her lawyer.

Today is probably the first time since we have all been together that me and Spud have read the newspaper when Tone was done with it. I don't know if I told you but I only read the paper when it concerns me. Well this doesn't concern me directly but after seeing what the article was about I was willing to make an exception.

Both Jennifer and the black dude she had been rolling with faces were on the front of the paper. According to the headlines they were both being accused of murder. Inside the paper the article told how the body of a suspected drug dealer had been discovered in his apartment with two shots to his head. There was a lot of bullshit in the article but what I did know was that the cops were saying that the black guy pulled the trigger and that he was seen leaving the crime scene.

There was no mention of anyone seeing or identifying Jennifer and then I found out how they had gotten her. The cops caught the black guy who in turn told on Jennifer as soon as he was at the Homicide Unit. He told the cops that it was all Jennifer's idea to rob the guy and that he hadn't actually pulled the trigger. He told the cops that him and the victim struggled for the gun and it fell then Jennifer picked it up and shot him twice.

I knew what was next so I read on waiting to see what Jennifer had said but to my surprise she ain't say nothing. If what the paper was reporting was true then she didn't make no statement at all. I couldn't believe this shit. She had stood tall even though the nigga she had been rocking with folded. I closed the paper and noticed that the paper was two days old which meant that if dude wasn't already in the jail he was surely on his way. I had big plans for the nigga. I told Spud what I was thinking and he agreed as did Tone. Just like that main man's fate had been sealed and now it was only a matter of waiting.

* * * * *

That was the first statement then there was a second one.

* * * * *

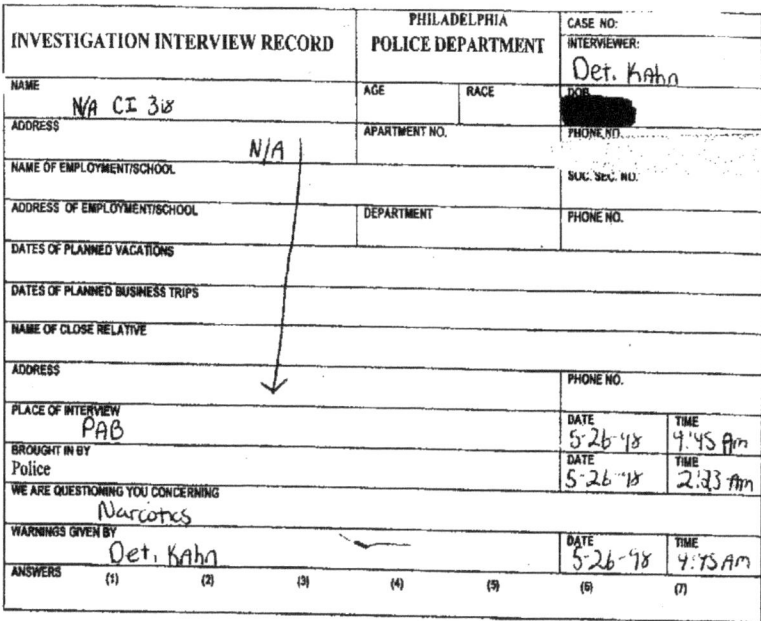

Q. Do you understand why you are here?

A. Yes I am here to give you information on a drug organization.

Q. And are you doing this because earlier this morning you swerved your car and were pulled over by a patrol officer who after searching your car found an ounce of heroin?

A. Yes.

Q. Were you subsequently charged with DUI and possession of narcotics?

A. Yes.

Q. Do you understand that any leniency you may receive will be dependent upon how valuable the information you give us is?

A. I do.

Q. You claim to have info on a organization that we have been investigating correct?

A. Yes.

Q. Who are the heads of this organization?

A. Pooh, Tone and Spud.

Q. By Pooh, Tone and Spud do you mean Darnell Nevins, Anthony Serrano and Alexus Rios?

A. Yes.

| INVESTIGATION INTERVIEW RECORD | CITY OF PHILADELPHIA |
| CONTINUATION SHEET | POLICE DEPARTMENT |

NAME: CI 318 **PAGE:** 1 **CASE NO.**

Q. I have already informed you that we have extensive information on them but you claim to have information that I am not aware of what information is that?

A. I know that they are selling weight.

Q. When you say they are selling weight you mean they are wholesaling correct?

A. Right.

Q. How do you know this?

A. I bought some from them.

Q. Is that where the ounce of heroin in your car came from?

A. Yes.

Q. Which one of the three men in question did you purchase the heroin from?

A. Anthony.

Q. Anthony Serrano?

A. Yes.

Q. I told you that we want to use an undercover cop to purchase narcotics from these three but and you say that there is only one way to do that. How is that?

Q. You have to go through Spud.

Q. You mean Alexus?

A. Yes.

Q. Alright what do we do?

A. Pooh or Tone will never deal with your undercover you will have to target Spud he is the greed one.

Q. You know I've been investigating these guys for a long time and I have never heard of them selling weight are you sure your information is accurate?

A. I'm positive I told you I got the ounce in my car from Anthony.

INVESTIGATION INTERVIEW RECORD CONTINUATION SHEET	CITY OF PHILADELPHIA POLICE DEPARTMENT
NAME CI 318	PAGE　CASE NO.

Q. How were you able to purchase your drugs?

A. I've been with them since the beginning they trust me but they won't trust your cop.

Q. If you have it so good with them why don't you buy for me?

A. Because I like my life.

Q. What does that mean?

A. It means that if they were to even ever suspect that I was setting them up they would kill me without hesitation. If they find out your officer is a cop he'll still get to live I won't.

Q. Are they really that violent?

A. Yes.

Q. Do you think our officer will get harmed?

A. I don't think so I think they're smart enough not to kill a cop.

Q. So getting in through this Spud guy is our best option?

A. Yes.

Q. Okay we'll try it and if it works we will make arrangements to dispose of your case understood?

A. I understand.

APHILLYATION & 5 STAR SCRIBES PUBLISHING PRESENTS

That was the first statement then there was a second one.

INVESTIGATION INTERVIEW RECORD	PHILADELPHIA POLICE DEPARTMENT	CASE NO: N/A INTERVIEWER: Det. Kahn	
NAME N/A CI 318	AGE N/A	RACE N/A	DOB ▓▓▓
ADDRESS	APARTMENT NO.	PHONE NO.	
NAME OF EMPLOYMENT/SCHOOL		SOC. SEC. NO.	
ADDRESS OF EMPLOYMENT/SCHOOL	DEPARTMENT	PHONE NO.	
DATES OF PLANNED VACATIONS			
DATES OF PLANNED BUSINESS TRIPS			
NAME OF CLOSE RELATIVE			
ADDRESS		PHONE NO.	
PLACE OF INTERVIEW PAB		DATE 4-04-00	TIME 3:00pm
BROUGHT IN BY Police		DATE 4-04-00	TIME 2:30pm
WE ARE QUESTIONING YOU CONCERNING An ongoing investigation			
WARNINGS GIVEN BY N/A		DATE	TIME
ANSWERS (1) (2) (3)	(4) (5)	(6)	(7)

Q I have explained to you why you are back here have I not?
A. You have.
Q. Almost two years ago we acted upon a tip that you gave us but as of yet we have netted no results do you know why that is?
A. No.
Q. We have been buying ounces for almost two years and we have nothing to show for it now if you can't do something to help us you will be going to jail for that ounce you had in your car. What more can you give us?
A. If you've gone through Spud and got nothing there is only one other suggestion I can give to you.
Q. What is that?
A. You have to up your buy.
Q. Why would we do that?
A. Because your not getting their attention with the buys you're making. If you up your buy it will get their attention.
Q. What are you talking about?
A. If someone buys the same amount of product all the time then they switch and they up their purchase by a lot it makes the seller wonder. The first two things they suspect is a cop and the second is a robbery. If they suspect a robbery all three will show up to protect their product and each other if that happenes you will get them all in the same place with the drugs.
Q.

INVESTIGATION INTERVIEW RECORD CONTINUATION SHEET	CITY OF PHILADELPHIA POLICE DEPARTMENT
NAME CT 318	PAGE / CASE NO.

Q. What makes you think that will work?

A. It's what I would do.

Q. What does that mean?

A. I sold drugs for a long time and if somebody upped their purchase on me and I suspected a robbery I would show up to protect my product.

Q. You wouldn't suspect a cop if someone upped their purchase like you're saying we should do?

A. Not if they been buying as long as you have. You have been buying a while and there has been no police heat on them.

Q. So you're saying that you wouldn't suspect a cop if it were you?

A. Not from a steady customer but I would suspect a robbery.

Q. We'll see. If we come up short our deal is off understood?

A. I understand. Make sure your cop doesn't wear a wire on his chest or nuts because they are the first places they will check.

Q. How do you know that?

A. That's drug dealing 101.

All three of us read the statements twice then the questions began to come and I am first to ask one.

"Tone who'd you sell an ounce to around dat time?"

"I ain't sell no ounces to nobody."

"Da statement say you did."

"Don't none of our outlets even buy ounces every-body cop more den dat," Tone says.

"Is we even sure dis shit is right?" Spud asks pointing at the statements in my hand.

"Why wouldn't it be?" I ask him.

"Well if it's right we gotta know whoeva it is," Spud says.

"Why you say dat?" Tone questions.

"Because whoeva told on us said dey been wit us from da beginning."

"It's Los," Tone said automatically.

"Los ain't know we was sellin weight."

Tone and Spud continue to go back and forth throwing names around. I blocked them out for a minute and re-read the statements. This time I am more focused and notice a few things that catch my attention. Certain things that the CI said lets me know that it is definitely somebody close to us. I reread the statements again and this time something else catches my eye. This time it's the date and times on the first statement. Those times, along with something the detective asks the CI jars my memory.

I'm not sure what I am trying to remember until I look at the time again and realize that the times mean that it had just turned May 26th.

Whatever I was trying to remember would have nothing to do with May 26th. It would have to do with May 25th. Immediately that date is extremely familiar to me and it only takes me a few seconds to figure out why. As soon as I figure out why a chill runs through my body. I look at the statements again and I notice something else. Then I noticed something else and this trend continues.

The more I look at the statements the more I begin to notice certain things that point to a certain person causing more chills to run through me. It isn't until I get to the end of the second statement that all is validated to me and I figure out who told on us.

The moment I realize who it is I begin to feel sick to my stomach. I feel betrayed like never before. I would never guess in a million years that this person would have told on us. I put all my faith in this person and it was killing me that I was even thinking that they betrayed my trust. I probably would have stayed in my trance if I didn't hear something that Tone said.

"What you just say?" I ask Tone.

"I know who told on us," he responds.

"So do I," I tell him.

"It's Bebe," he says.

"No, it ain't," I tell him.

"Pooh I know dats ya young bul and all dat but we gotta look at dis for what it is."

"I am and I'm tellin you it's not Bebe."

"If it ain't him, who is it den?"

"It's Rosie."

"What? Nigga you trippin. My aunt ain't no rat."

"Just hear me out dog. I don't wanna believe it neither but it's true."

"Prove it," Tone tells me and I set about doing that.

"First off, look at da dates and times on da first statement. It say dat da CI was pulled over wit a ounce of dope in dey car on da 26th after swerving dey car at two in da morning. I ain't catch it da first time cause it said da 26th but when you think about it, to us two in da morning is still da 25th and what's da 25th?" I ask looking at Tone and Spud who both shrug their shoulders.

"How da fuck I'm pose to know?" Tone asks.

"You know. You just ain't focused on it but dats Rosie's birthday. Remember when she left da club dat night she was drunk as shit. Den when she pulled off she was drivin all crazy swerving and shit and she had a ounce of dope on her dat she got from Anthony. Whoeva made da statement called you Anthony. Ain't nobody else goin call you Anthony. Everybody else call you Tone."

"Whoeva made da statement said dey brought da dope from me," Tone says to me.

"Dat was a lie, probably to make da cops believe her."

"I don't know dog. You could still be wrong."

"Alight how bout dis whoeva made da statement said dat Spud was da greedy one. Who else but us know dat Spud greedy. And whoeva made da statement said dey been wit us since da beginning and Rosie da only one dat been wit us since den. But if dat don't convince you den just look at da second page of da second statement. It say dat da first places we would check for wires is da chest and da nuts den dey ask da CI how dey know dat and da CI say dats drug dealing 101."

I see the expression on Tone's face change and I know why. The drug dealing 101 statement brought back a memory for him just like it did for me. Back when we first got the case working jobs and Rosie was schooling me she told me to always check for wires when I was doing big business with someone. When she told me this she had looked at Tone and asked him what that action was called and he responded that it was drug dealing 101. That was the line she used when she broke down the basics of the drug game. She had done it with Tone in Puerto Rico and she had done it with me in Philly.

The cell grows extremely silent and Tone reaches for the statements. I hand them to him and he reads them again. When he finishes he shakes his head and I know that he is beginning to see what I see. He is beginning to see that we have been sold out by the one person we thought we could trust wholeheartedly. The woman who had been like a mother to both of us is the same one who gave us up to the cops.

"She was goin retire," Tone says.

"What?" I ask.

"She was goin retire. Remember she told us dat on her birthday?"

"Yeah so?"

"Dats why she told on us. Remember when she was talkin she was talkin bout enjoyin her money and how she couldn't go to jail for life. She said she couldn't even go to jail for ten years. She was scared of da time she was goin get for dat ounce so she gave us up," Tone states.

That was exactly what she had said and hearing Tone say it makes me know that he believes me. He puts his head down and looks at the floor. I look at Spud who has a look on his face that I can't read.

"What you thinkin bout?" I ask him.

"Dis shit crazy. Dat bitch told on us."

"I know. Now we gotta figure out what we goin do bout it," I tell him.

Chapter 17

DECEMBER 2001

C.F.C.F UNIT D2-1

It has been a crazy week and not once during that week have we been to court. Allow me to tell you what's been going on. As you know we had been given a day off from court by the judge. On that day I received the statements of the person who had gave us up to the cops who we determined was Rosie. Once we found this out there was a lot of emotions involved because of who she was and what she had done for us but one thing we all knew was that something had to be done. We discussed this for hours even though we all knew that Rosie had to die. We knew she had to die. We just weren't sure in which manner she should die.

We had another discussion and finally we came to an agreement and just like that her fate was sealed. I called Bebe that night and told him to make sure that he came to see me the following day when I returned from court and he said he would be there. The next day we went to court and sat through the opening statements and questioning of a few witnesses then court was recessed for the day.

Bebe was at the jail that night and when I went on my visit I told him what we had discovered and what we needed him to do. I gave him strict instructions on what was to be done and he simply said that he would take care of it. When I got back to the block that night I told Tone and Spud about the visit with Bebe and they said nothing which I understood. I was feeling just like they were. I wished I didn't have to do what we were doing but it had to be done. Rosie had brought this on herself.

The following morning instead of being called for court with the other inmates we were woken up and taken to the receiving room where instead of sheriffs there were Homicide Detectives waiting for us. The minute I saw this I knew that Bebe had taken care of business. We were at the Homicide Unit for two days being questioned by the detectives who thought they could get something out of us. While we were there I even got a chance to meet Detective Kahn who was the cop that Rosie gave her statement to.

He was more pissed off than everybody. For hours he cursed and called me every name in the book while asking me how I had found out the identity of his confidential informant but all I did was laugh. When they finally got tired they shipped us back to the county jail. As soon as we got back to the unit we fully understood why they were so mad. Bebe had gone a little too far.

When I got to my cell there was a newspaper laying on my bed and the article made me understand why there was so much outrage. All Bebe was supposed to do was kill Rosie then call Detective Kahn from a pay phone and tell him where to find the body. I had mailed the statement to Bebe to leave with the body so when Kahn found her he would know exactly why it had happened but it went a little further than expected.

According to the newspaper Rosie's body had been found in front of the courthouse with multiple gunshots to her face and head. The statements had been affixed to her chest courtesy of a nail gun and to top it all off a dead rat had been stuffed in her mouth. The article also said that a reporter had been the one to discover the body. It was reported that an anonymous call was made to the reporter informing her of the dead body laying in front of the courthouse. After reading the article I immediately called Bebe and talking in code I asked him what had happened. In not so many words he told me that Rosie got what she deserved and all I could do was smile because he was right. She did get what she deserved. She ratted on us and had been dealt with accordingly.

We are supposed to go back to court tomorrow and I hope we do because I am ready to get this shit over with. The trial should be over relatively quick because that is the way we want it. We have a game plan. Our lawyers are being paid for one thing and one thing only and that is to save us from the death penalty. We'll see what happens.

* * * * *

DECEMBER 2001

CRIMINAL JUSTICE CENTER (CJC)

13TH & FILBERT

TWO WEEKS LATER

The last time I spoke to you I was telling you about the incident with Rosie and at the end of all that I told you that we were going back to court, well we did. We went back to court and after the discovery of Rosie's body the rest of our trial has been like a circus. There has been arguments in the courtroom. Accusations have been thrown at us from everyone and throughout it all we've done nothing but smile.

To most on the outside looking in our trial looked like a sham. There were a lot of witnesses presented by the prosecution but our lawyers barely questioned any of them. When they did question them it was to simply make it look like they were doing something when they really weren't. We didn't care about the trial. All we cared about was the penalty phase which we had just gone through.

My bad I forgot to tell you, we were found guilty three days ago. The jury only deliberated for what has to be a record ten minutes before returning with a verdict of guilty. I mean it's not like it was that hard. We were recorded during the killing. The verdict came back so fast that the sheriffs didn't even have enough time to take us back down to the cells.

The trial may have looked like a pushover but the penalty phase was something different altogether. Our lawyers put their legal prowess on display bringing forth witnesses to testify on our behalf and tearing the prosecution's witnesses to shreds. It all sounds good, right? Don't let it fool you, the recording of the killing hurt us so much that I'd be surprised if they didn't kill us right there in the courtroom. My lawyer already told me that the chances of me getting the death penalty are great so I have prepared myself for that.

My only solace is that me and my brothers stood up like men and took it on the chin. None of us told to save our ass nor did we take any deal. I look at Tone and Spud and there is no fear in their eyes, there is no remorse. All there is is fearlessness. They both know what's coming and the looks on their faces says come on with it.

The sheriff comes to the cell and opens the door then calls our names. We all stand and follow him to the elevator which leads us to the floor our courtroom is located on. The sheriff leads us into the courtroom and I notice that there are more sheriffs in attendance than usual. The added sheriff presence tells me that it wasn't looking good for us. They were there to make sure that we didn't get crazy when the jury delivered our fate. Speaking of the jury, they are being brought into the courtroom so I'll holla at y'all later and let y'all know what happened.

* * * * *

Un-fucking believable! I've heard of miracles before but never believed in them and I definitely never thought I would be on the receiving end of one but I was today as were my brothers. I know it sounds strange for someone to say that life in prison is a good thing but it beats being sentenced to death. The jury rejected the death penalty for all of us and gave us all life without parole.

I'm going to be 100% truthful with you. I don't know how this happened. I had already prepared myself for the death penalty and I'm sure Tone and Spud had too but it didn't happen. When the judge announced our sentence there was outrage and relief being displayed all around us and it almost turned into a zoo. There were curses from the cops, family and friends and sighs of exasperation from the prosecution. It was as if no one in the entire courtroom could figure out how this had happened.

I tried to find an explanation but I couldn't. It

might have been the testimony of Lisette and Becca and the tears they shed or it could have been how our lawyers explained to the jury how all we had ever known was the streets. Maybe it was the way my lawyer slid it in that the woman who had initially set us up by the cops was the same woman who introduced us into the life we now lived or maybe it was God.

That last one intrigued me the most because it was something I had never considered before or even cared about for that matter. My celly is a holy roller and every once in a while he tries to convert me but is never successful. He told me that if I prayed that everything would be alright. For the past three days I have found myself whispering prayers to God, asking him to spare me and my brothers from the death penalty. I don't know if that is what spared us but I'm leaning towards that being the reason. I know we should have been facing execution but we're not. We're going to live albeit in jail forever, but we're still going to live. I'll still see my kids grow up.

If my prayers were what saved us then that might be something I'd consider doing more often. I never thought that God would answer the prayers of a nigga like me but maybe it is like my celly said it was. Maybe God is merciful. I don't know what's going on but what I do know is this. For some reason or another I was spared today.

'The sheriffs quickly removed us from the crowded courtroom filled with mixed emotions that range from relieved to pissed the fuck off. Once we are back in the cell we celebrate our minor victory until we are herded on the sheriff's bus heading back to the jail. On the bus though we become serious because we know there is one more piece of serious business that we have to take care of and we know we have to do it quick. It has to be done quick because when we get back we'll only be in population for a few hours before we are taken to the hole to await our trip upstate. We already know what we have to do and we plan on doing it right. When we're done it will just be one more thing for people to talk about when they mention our names.

* * * * *

"How long before dey come get us and take us to da hole?" I ask Mi-Mi as soon as we get back on the block.

"Sometime after count. What happened?"

"We got life," I say and turn to walk away from the desk.

"Where you goin? I wanna talk to you."

"I'll be back in a lil while. I gotta take care of some business."

"Pooh," she calls out to me and I turn around to face her.

"What's up?"

"Don't fuck him up too bad."

"I can't promise you dat sweetheart. He bought dis shit."

I walk to Tone and Spud's cell. They are smoking cigarettes when I get there. We talk for a few minutes about what we have to do then when they are done with their cigarettes we exit the cell. I look around the dayroom until I spot who I am looking for. I tell Tone and Spud to chill while I go set shit in motion.

The nigga that I spotted when we first came out of the cell is the nigga that told on Jennifer. He's been in the jail for a while now but I just had him moved onto the block courtesy of Mi-Mi. We had pondered fucking him up when he first came in the jail but we didn't want to run the risk of getting split up before our trial was over. Now that we're on our way out of here it don't matter anymore. Dude gotta pay for telling on Becca's sister and it ain't no getting around that.

Mi-Mi had the strings pulled to have him moved on the block two weeks ago and as soon as he arrived I got cool with him. It was easy seeing as how dude was joe as shit. I smoked a few cigarettes with him and a little bit of weed and just like I figured, in no time he was acting like I was his best friend. He looks at me as I am approaching and smiles.

"Pooh what's up baby? What happened?"

"Dey gave me a wheel."

"Damn, dats crazy."

"Dat shit ain't bout nothin. You tryin to go blow?"

"Hell, yeah nigga. I been fienin all day."

"Come on den. Let's go to ya cell," I say and he leads the way.

I follow him to his cell and Tone and Spud follow me. This is the same setup we used with Stiz when we found out that he was a rat. The only difference this time is there won't be any time between us entering the cell and fucking him up like there was with Stiz.

As soon as he enters the cell I step in right behind him. He turns around and I sucka punch him. He backs up a little but I advance towards him swinging as hard as I can. I land two or three good shots before he goes down to one knee and curls up.

By this time Tone and Spud are in the cell and the door is locked. Spud immediately rushes over to him and kicks him in the head numerous times. When the nigga lifts his head, Spud catches him square in his face and his head snaps back. His eyes roll back into his head and he collapses onto his back and begins whimpering.

"What's dis about?" he asks weakly.

"You told on da wrong bitch homie."

"I ain't tell on nobody."

"You ain't tell on Jennifer?" I ask and he doesn't respond. "Dats what I thought," I say, then begin to stomp him.

Tone and Spud join in and we stomp him for about two

minutes. When we stop, his head is split, his face is swollen and he is missing a few teeth. There is blood all over the floor and he is just laying there moaning in pain. Tone, who already knows what to do begins to search the cell until he finds the niggas phone book.

"I got it right here," Tone tells me.

"Find da address," I tell him and he searches the book.

"Got it," he says as he hands me the book showing me where the address is.

"You can hear me, right?" I ask him as I kneel next to him but he doesn't answer.

I grab a shower shoe that is laying next to him and smack him in the face with it. The sound of the hard plastic hitting skin is loud in the small cell. "I asked you a question. Can you hear me?"

"Yeah," he responds lowly.

"Good cause you don't wanna miss what I'ma say. I got ya mom's address and if you love her den you goin do what I say. Tomorrow you goin call whoeva ya lawyer is and tell him you want to meet wit da Homicide Detectives. When you meet wit em you goin tell em you lied when you said dat

Jennifer killed da nigga. If you don't my man on da streets goin kill ya mom. Afta you meet wit da detectives Jennifer's lawyer goin come see you and you goin tell him da same thing you told da detectives. If you don't my man goin kill ya mom. When you go to trial you goin get on da stand and tell da jury da same thing you told da detectives and her lawyer. If you try anything otha den what I said you know what's goin happen. If you know who I am den you know I ain't playin. Make dis shit right or lose ya mother understand?"

"Man, I can't . . ."

"You can't what?" I ask and smack him in the face with the shower shoe again.

"Aah shit! Aiight man, I'll do it."

"Make sure you do. I'm callin my youngin tonight and givin him dis address so if you try to move ya mom, he goin kill her on sight. Please don't try me. Matter of fact I'ma keep dis whole phone book for insurance. Please don't try me."

"I'ma take care of it dog, I swear. Just don't hurt my mom, please."

"Dats up to you," I say and kick him in his face again.

"Stay da fuck in dis hut tonight too," I say before we turn and exit the cell.

Mi-Mi is watching us as we come out of the cell but I pay her no attention. I go straight to my hut and call Bebe. I give him the address and tell him that I'll send him a letter telling him what it's about. We talk for a few minutes about a few things but the day's court proceedings never come up. Finally I end the call and the call for count comes over the intercom. Knowing that this means that my time on the block is getting shorter I begin to pack my shit so I'm ready when they come to get me.

* * * * *

As soon as count cleared, Daniels calls my celly for a visit then buzzes the door. While he is getting ready I tell Daniels to open Tone and Spud's cell. When she does I give them the phone so they can make a few calls, then go back to my cell. I close the door and sit down thinking about all that has transpired. I am in such a trance that I don't hear my door when it buzzes again. It isn't until Mi-Mi is standing in my doorway that I snap out of it. She comes into the cell and pulls the door but doesn't lock it.

"Where's ya curtain?" she asks.

"What?"

"Where ya curtain at?"

"What is you doin?" I ask.

"Just hurry up and put da curtain up."

I grab the towel and toothbrush that I use to cover the window of my cell and put it up so that no one can see in.

When I look back to Mi-Mi she is undoing the belt around her waist and I look at her like she is crazy.

"You trippin yo. You goin lose ya job if we get caught."

"We ain't goin get caught."

"Who in da bubble?"

"My girlfriend."

"Which one?"

"Da same one who be in da school building."

"You sure bout dis?"

"Yeah I'm sure. You ain't think I was goin let you go upstate without givin you one last shot of dis pussy did you?"

She finally undoes her belt and the button on her pants. She pulls them down to her ankles and sticks her finger into her pussy. I watch for a few seconds as she plays with herself then she takes her finger out and licks her juices off. She smiles slyly and puts her hands on the table poking her ass and pussy out at me. Instantly I pull my dick out and walk up behind her. I play with her pussy for a few seconds myself then I position myself to slide up in her.

I place my dick at her pussy and after two attempts I feel myself sliding in. Once I am all the way in I begin to pump slowly at first but Mi-Mi obviously has other things in mind.

"I don't want it like dat Pooh. Fuck me hard and fast give me somethin to remember."

She ain't even got to say no more. I grab her by the waist and start to pound her as fast and as hard as I can. She moans but not loud enough for anyone to hear and these moans drive me crazy. I pound away at her pussy knowing that it might be the last shot that I have in a while. Her moans tell me that she is loving every minute of it. I feel myself about to cum and even though I don't believe it is possible I go faster. Mi-Mi must sense what is about to happen because she begins to grind her ass back into me and that's all it takes.

I cum with a fury burying my seed deep inside her. I keep my dick in her until every drop is out of me then I slide out of her. As soon as I do she turns to face me and kisses me furiously. We kiss for about a minute and when she pulls her lips away she keeps her face close to mine, so close in fact that our lips are almost still touching.

"I been wantin to feel you cum in me for a long time."

"Well now you got it."

"Don't worry I'm on da pill."

"It's cool."

"I love you Pooh. I know you think I'm lyin and da last time I said it you ain't say it back so you ain't gotta say it now but it's true. I love you and I'ma be there for you whenvea you need me to be whether you believe dat or not."

When she was done speaking she grabbed the toilet paper and wiped herself off. She handed me the toilet paper then pulled her pants up. When she had herself back in order she turned to head out da door but I stopped her by calling her name. She turns to face me and I smile a gesture she returns. "I love you too sweetheart," I tell her.

"I knew you did," she says and exits the cell.

Epilogue

MARCH 2002

STATE CORRECTIONAL INSTITUTION

AT CAMP HILL A-BLOCK

This will be the last time that you hear from me, I am officially done talking about anything that has occurred prior to me coming upstate. Since I have told you my whole story I will update you on what has happened the last three months then I will be done with it. The first thing I will address is the situation with Jennifer since it is freshest in my mind.

Jennifer went to her preliminary hearing and her rat ass co-defendant did what he was supposed to. Better yet what he had to. He made the statement saying that he had lied to the detectives.

During this hearing Jennifer was still held over for trial but her lawyer says that if her co-defendant gets on the stand at trial and says what he said in his new statement then Jennifer should be alright. I got a letter from her the other day thanking me for what we had done but I didn't respond. Hopefully every-thing works out for her.

Bebe is still doing his thing. I get weekly updates from him on how things are going and he keeps in constant contact with Lisette. He talks to her at least once a day making sure that her and the kids are alright but this doesn't surprise me. I always knew that in my absence he would fill my shoes properly. I heard word that he just caught another homicide and when I asked him about it he simply told me that it had to be done so I left it alone. Sometimes shit gotta be done.

Lisette and the kids are doing good all things considered. She's holding on like the soldier that I know she is. Even though I am upstate she still comes to see me faithfully like I was still down the county. I know it's hard on her so I tell her that she doesn't have to come all the time but she does anyway and I know that this will continue as long as she is able.

Ronnie now lives in Pennsylvania. Actually she's not too far from the jail I'm at. I told her that I would only be here for a few months but she claims she doesn't care and I don't think that she does. A nigga couldn't ask for a better mistress. She is already plotting on how to get pregnant by me in the visiting room. I told her to wait until I get to another jail because I've heard that it's sweeter at other jails. I know I said that I didn't want anymore kids but if anyone deserves for me to go against my word it's her. So it looks like I'm not only goin to be a daddy again but also spending some nice time in the hole. My only problem is how to explain to Lisette how my visits got taken away. I'll figure out something.

Mi-Mi is still around, I get at least two letters from her every week. She says she wants to come visit me but between Lisette and Ronnie I'm not sure how I'm going to work this out. I told her that she has to wait and she says she'll be patient until I can figure something out. In the meantime we'll just have to continue communicating through letters. I just got a letter from her and in that letter was some thong shots of her which will surely help me to remember her.

Spud is cool. We on the same block. He back in his jail bag. The other day when I talked to Lisette she told me to tell Spud that Becca said for him to call her. I told him and he said he would but who knows with him.

Tone on the other hand is in the hole where he has been for the last month and a half. Tone who was also on the block with us went to the hole for fucking his celly up. Tone had already told me that he didn't like the nigga and one night he fucked him up real bad. When the guard came around he thought Tone had killed him but he was just knocked out. I hope we end up at our home jails together because I know he will make my time go faster.

Other than that it's the same old shit and I ain't doing

nothing but preparing myself for the long haul ahead of me. I am fortunate enough to not have been sentenced to death and I plan on doing everything I can to be the best father that I can be from behind these walls.

I'm officially done folks. This will be the last time you hear from me unless I get a pardon. I did everything I could and I'm not as mad as people might think. Of course I'm mad that I'm in jail but I knew that this was a strong possibility when I was doing all the shit I did. I made a lot of money and I had fun doing it so it wasn't all a waste. I do know one thing though. Me and my brothers left our mark on Da Bad Landz and can't nobody say otherwise. If they try to, they liars.

Da Bad Landz ain't what it used to be because it ain't the right caliber of niggas out there but all that is about to change and it's all because of one nigga. I got a letter from Teddy a while ago through Lisette and he was telling me that he was about to hit the streets. He told me about his plans for when he hits the streets and after reading the letter all I could do was pray for whoever gets in his way. I've heard the stories of who's doing what on the streets but all of that don't mean shit. A true boss is getting ready to hit the streets and when he does it's going to be a whole new ball game. Excuse me for a minute. My mail just came under the door.

FIVE MINUTES LATER

You know that it's been years since I have cried for any reason. My mom died and I didn't cry. I killed my pop and never batted an eye but the news I just got in the letter I received breaks my heart. Since I have told you so much already and you're familiar with everybody I hold dear in my heart, I will share this with you and be done. I just got a letter from Lisette and she told me that my youngin Bebe has been killed. I couldn't believe it at first but then I had to realize that death is a part of the life that Bebe lived. I cried for a minute or two when she told me because it was like her telling me that my own son had been killed but now I have pulled myself together. I just wanted to share that with you before I ended this.

There are only two ways that you will ever hear from me again. One is if they ever slip up and let me go. The other is if I ever get my hands on the nigga that killed Bebe. If either of those things ever happen, I'll get with you because once again I will have a story to tell.

If you liked Pooh. You'll love Teddy.

BE ON THE LOOKOUT FOR:

The Teddy Trilogy

HONOR, BETRAYAL & RETRIBUTION

PRESENTED BY

APHILLYATION & 5 STAR SCRIBES PUBLISHING

ABOUT THE AUTHOR

Authentic is an author who is currently serving a life sentence. From the confines of his cell he reaches out delivering stories that are gritty, raw and so believable you'll feel like you live them personally. Only an author who has lived what he writes about can make you feel that way. Authentic is that author. He has taken real life experience, pain and passion, laced it with a tone of creativity and transformed the genre that fans love into something new. Welcome to the era of "FICTIONALIZED REALITY." It's a new day.

Authentic welcomes feedback from readers and can be contacted by e-mail at: 5starscribespublishing@gmail.com